Accessible Access 2000

Springer
London
Berlin
Heidelberg
New York
Barcelona
Hong Kong
Milan
Paris
Singapore
Tokyo

Accessible Access 2000

Mark Whitehorn and Bill Marklyn

 Springer

Mark Whitehorn
Information Technology Services, University College Worcester,
Henwick Grove, Worcester WR2 6AJ, UK

Bill Marklyn
OceanPark Software Corporation, 2332 E Aloha Street
Seattle WA 98112, USA

ISBN 1-85233-313-8 Springer-Verlag London Berlin Heidelberg

British Library Cataloguing in Publication Data
Whitehorn, Mark, 1953-
  Accessible Access 2000
  1.Microsoft Access 2000 (Computer file)
  I.Title II.Marklyn, Bill, 1960-
  005.7'565

  ISBN 1852333138

Library of Congress Cataloging-in-Publication Data
Whitehorn, Mark, 1953-
  Accessible Access 2000 / Mark Whitehorn and Bill Marklyn.
    p. cm.
  ISBN1-85233-313-8 (alk. paper)
    1. Microsoft Access (Computer file) 2. Database management. I. Marklyn, Bill, 1960-
  II. Title

QA76.9.D3 W482 2000
005.75'65--dc21   00-032976

Typeset by Ian Kingston Editorial Services, Nottingham
Printed and bound at The Cromwell Press, Trowbridge, Wiltshire, England
34/3830-543210 Printed on acid-free paper SPIN 10766488

This book is dedicated to

Pamela Mary Barham

(née Moulton),

who always meant to write a book,

but spent too much time on other people

ever to get around to it.

Acknowledgements

Top of the list has to be Mary Whitehorn, who contributed so much that by rights she should have been listed as another author, but she declined on the grounds of modesty (now that **is** rare in a writer).

Also up there are those ever-cheerful people at Springer Verlag – Beverley Ford, Rebecca Mowat and Sally Tickner who all worked hard behind the scenes and provided the drive and enthusiasm.

And finally, grateful thanks are due to the Three Crowns at Ullingswick. This tranquil establishment (with superb food) was where we planned the early stages of the project. Of course, as work progressed, further restorative visits were unavoidable....

Contents

Part III – Creating hand-crafted databases   75

Part I

Introduction

Chapter 1

Introduction

This is where we try to convince you to buy the book, tell you what it tries to do, define a few terms and generally set the scene – all of which makes this more like an introduction than a first chapter, but no-one reads introductions so we called it a chapter. If you have already bought the book and know what it does, feel free to skip to Chapter 2 where the action starts.

Why should you buy this book?

There are many Access books on the market, why should I buy this one? Does it have more information than any other book?

Errr, no, it actually has less than the big reference books you'll also find on the shelf.

So, is it very cheap?

Well, it isn't as expensive as some but, no, it isn't particularly cheap either.

To be brutally frank, you're not doing a great job of selling this to me.

Right, time for the hard sell.

Bill Marklyn worked for Microsoft as the Development Manager for the first three versions of Access. I (Mark) write the database column for *Personal Computer World* in the UK, build databases for a living and also teach database theory and practice.

We met (at a database conference, not unreasonably, given our interests) in the summer before Access 1.0 was launched and found that we shared similar views on how databases should be designed and built. Since then we have written a book together about the relational model that underlies Access and all other relational database systems (see below for the inevitable plug). But why write a book about Access itself when there are already so many around?

Well, since Bill was in charge of the product's development, it was fair to assume that we had the technical side reasonably well covered. I have been teaching people (students and IT professionals) to use Access since version 1.0 appeared and found that teaching it was very different from teaching a package like Word.

When you teach someone how to use Word, you find that you can spend most of your time concentrating on how to use the features that Word offers. You don't need to tell them what a letter is, or a paragraph, or italics; they already know all that.

Access is a tool that lets you create databases and, in my experience, most people, including IT professionals, who come on an Access course have never built a database before. (The people who have experience with building databases often simply pick up Access and start work with it, so I rarely saw them.)

The people who do come on courses tend to know that databases are used to store data but the detail beyond that is usually hazy. So I found that I needed to teach them about the features that Access offers and at the same time teach them how use that knowledge to create a database. To give a concrete example, I would show them how to build a table and also tell them what a table did within a database. And when I taught them how to build a form I also told them how the form would be used in a database and how forms could interact with tables.

So when Bill and I planned this Access book, we had two very specific aims. We wanted it to tell you:

- how to get started with Access as rapidly as possible.
- how to use a particular set of features effectively and also why those features are important.

Ah, but which features to show you? We were also aware that Access is, to coin a phrase, a very feature-rich product. This is vital because building and managing databases can become a complex operation. But at the start it doesn't **have** to be. We have endeavoured to focus on the parts that are fundamental. After all, you are going to have to learn not just how to drive Access but also what all of the components are for. You don't want to be sidetracked right at the start into learning features that you may not need for years; indeed, that you may never need.

So one really strange end result of our design for the book is that we hope that you'll buy it, not for all of the Access detail that we have put in, but for all the bits we have left out. Considering that Bill was instrumental in designing Access, we really could have stuffed this book with a mass of information. Instead we tried very hard to use my experience of teaching

Access to describe just the core – enough information to get you up and running but with no extraneous detail.

But once you have finished this book and you want to go on, for example, to become a professional Access developer, how do you find all of those extra bits that we don't tell you? You buy one of those great 1000+ page reference books that are available; there are some very good ones out there. So why not simply buy one of those now and save the cost of this one? Because this one will give you the framework that you need in order to use the information that those books contain.

So what do we cover?

We start by introducing the basic components of a database – tables, forms, queries and reports. We show you how to create simple examples of each using the Access wizards where appropriate. Then we cover each of them again, only this time we show you how to hand-build them so that you can achieve more than you can using just the wizards.

By that stage you should be comfortable with creating a simple database which stores its data in a single table. However, 'real-world' databases typically use multiple tables. So we show you why you need multiple tables and then run through those four components one more time, showing you how they can be used to create really effective multi-table databases.

What don't we cover?

In this book we have tried, as we said, to act as intelligent filters. A computer manual gives you every bit of information that you could possibly ever need; we are trying to give you only the most commonly used information. As a good example, Access provides so-called Input Masks that you can use to control what information can be placed in a database. Input masks can be composed of three different parts. However, the last two are optional and are rarely used in practice, so when we tell you about input masks we only cover the first part in any detail. This isn't because we don't know about the last two or because they are never used. It is simply that you can get 95% of the functionality of an input mask by understanding the first element. We think that the trade off is a good one, and that it will help you to become productive much more rapidly. Another example is that Access offers a facility called globally unique identifiers. These are useful when you build databases in which some users will want to work on data when they are disconnected from a shared database – for example, travelling sales people. It is a really useful feature, but not one you are likely to build into your first couple of databases. So we tell you about it but don't go into the details.

We also don't cover the more advanced features like programming Access or using it to generate database on the web. We also don't cover, more than is absolutely necessary, the theory that underlies database design and operation. This is a practical book about how you use Access. However, as a blatant plug, if you find that you want to know more about the underlying theory and database design in general, take a look at *Inside Relational Databases – with examples in Access*, Whitehorn and Marklyn, Springer Verlag ISBN 3-540-76092-X.

How do we work?

As with our first book, I tend to write most of the actual words while Bill provides a wealth of information and enthusiasm, proof reading and generally he keeps me on track. Since only one of us is in charge of the keyboard at any one time it often feels more natural to write in the first person – 'I prefer this', 'I recommend that' and so on. Since both of us see the text, you can assume that we agree in general with the sentiments expressed, although paradoxically it may not always be exactly true. Consider the statement 'I get paid for developing Access applications and use wizards whenever I think that using one will save me time.' I (Mark) do indeed get paid for developing Access applications, Bill doesn't – he got paid for developing Access itself – but we both agree that wizards are a good place to start. At other times, we'll use 'we' when it happens to run off the keyboard more naturally, for example, 'we have included on the CD-ROM a file called...'.

Who are you?

You are a reasonably competent Windows and Office user who has no experience with Access. You want to be able to create and use a stand-alone database to store and track information.

Making these assumptions means we don't waste time (and words) going into endless detail about common Office operations like opening and saving files. Nor do we cover components that are common to both Office and Access, like, for instance, Graph.

So if you've already used Access (or another database system) to create multi-table databases that work effectively then, much as we'd like you to buy this book, we'd encourage you to buy one of the more detailed books.

What do you have?

We also presume you have Access installed on your computer. These days, the installation process is just another Windows task and we won't be walking you through it. We also assume that you have installed all of Access; if not, we recommend that you go back and install the missing bits. The only reason we say this is so that we don't have to keep on checking that you have installed the bits necessary for the different operations we show you.

Definitions

We don't want to load you down with lots of techno-babble but it is useful if we define a couple of terms before we start.

Database

A database is simply a collection of data. Nowadays the term tends to be used about computerized systems but the old cards which were used to classify and locate books in a library are a good example of a non-computerized database.

Relational DataBase Management System (RDBMS)

A database is a collection of data – perhaps a list of your customers, their addresses, fax numbers and so on. In order to keep the data in your database under control, you need software known as a DBMS. The DBMS is to a database what a word processor is to a letter. The former is the controlling software, the latter the data that it manipulates. Access is a DBMS. In fact, it is also a Relational DBMS, hence the acronym. The word Relational simply refers to the way in which the data in the database is organized and since almost all modern DBMSs are relational the R is almost superfluous but is still commonly used.

Database application

So, you can use Access (an RDBMS) to create one or more databases. You will also hear people talking about using Access to create 'database applications'. The distinction between a database and a database application is a relatively fine one. Technically a database is simply a collection of information. As soon as you start using Access (or any other RDBMS) to create a user interface that allows people to interact with the data, then you are creating a database application. In practice, the database and the database application tend to be written together in Access so the difference is not very apparent. However, it is more so with other RDBMSs, such as Oracle.

Sample files

The CD supplied with this book has a folder called `AccSamp`. Within that folder is a set of files that are the example files that we generate and use in the book. We suggest that you copy the entire folder to a convenient location on your hard disk.

On our first book we provided a CD-ROM which had a batch file to move the files. This was, we discovered, a big mistake. Some people really don't like having files automatically placed on their disks, they like to choose where the files go. So this time we are playing safe and letting you do it.

Use Windows Explorer to move the entire folder to the location of your choice. Since the files are stored on a CD-ROM they will be read only, even when they are moved. So select all of the files in the folder on your hard disk (highlight one of the files and press Ctrl-A), right click on them, select 'Properties' and deselect the 'Read Only' option.

All the `.mdb` file names start with `chap` and the chapter number. For many of the chapters, you'll find files called `chapXstart.mdb` and `chapXend.mdb`: these are the files with which you should start work if you're following the examples and the file you should end up with once the example is complete. Sometimes there are intermediate files within a chapter; for instance, in Chapter 12 there are four files:

```
chap12start.mdb
chap12reports.mdb
chap12start2.mdb
chap12end.mdb
```

Occasionally there is no `chapXstart` file in a chapter where you start from scratch and work towards a completed example.

What's in a name?

When it first appeared, Access was revolutionary in many ways – one was that it allowed you to including spaces in the names of objects like tables, forms etc. This is great because it enables you to give tables meaningful names like 'Orders received'. This was a major step forward compared to the PC-based DBMSs of the day such as dBASE which only allowed 8 characters and no spaces. However, as Access applications were developed and became successful, an unexpected problem occurred. Many Access applications became so successful that they were upgraded to client–server systems. (These are larger, more complex database applications where the data is held centrally and many people can use it at the same time. A typical example of client–server database software is a Microsoft product called SQL Server, another is IBM's DB2.) Sadly most of these client–server systems didn't (and many still don't) support names with spaces. The result was that considerable work was often necessary to upsize these Access applications.

The situation is now considerably better for two reasons.

- Access allows you to create applications that are, right from the start, SQL Server compatible – so that if you ever do want to upsize the application to SQL Server the process is trivial. This is done using the 'projects' which are discussed briefly in Chapter 21.
- Version 7.0 (and above) of SQL Server does support long names and even spaces in those names (though other client–server systems and earlier version of SQL Server do not.)

However, suppose you develop an Access application in the normal way (that is, you do not use a project file) and then you later discover that you want to move it to a client–server system. It may also turn out that you don't want to use SQL Server as the client–server system, in which case any long names and/or those with spaces are going to be a pain. So, our general advice is to keep names shorter rather than longer and not to use spaces. On the other hand, if you are developing a simple addressing database that you know will never be upsized, feel free to use any combination of characters and spaces that Access permits.

For clarity's sake we have chosen to ignore our own advice in this book and have used rather long names. This book is primarily a teaching aid and we felt that the gain in making things easier to follow was worthwhile.

Disclaimer

We've made every effort to ensure that the material in this book is accurate but we cannot guarantee that it works perfectly or that we haven't made mistakes (we are only human). If you find a problem with the book we'd love to know, so please tell us at www.penguinsoft.co.uk. You can also check out that site to see if we have posted any fixes for the material herein.

As a general rule, always work with a copy of your data when you're experimenting, developing or just simply playing. It's the simplest way to avoid problems and furthermore, knowing that you can't do any damage gives you greater confidence to experiment and learn by both your successes and your mistakes.

The 'd' word

Data: singular or plural? We know, correctly speaking, that datum is singular and data is plural. We also know that it sounds funny when used that way so we've gone with common usage and, with apologies to purists, merrily write 'data is' throughout.

Conventions and layout

This is a practical book so we continually tell you to type material into Access. Sometimes it seems clearer to use single inverted commas to outline exactly what we mean – for example, on page 49:

Thus 'car???' will find Carmel...

At other times we have left them out because they seem superfluous. As a general rule Access doesn't expect single inverted commas around the information that you type in.

Most people don't read books from cover to cover; so we have occasionally repeated important points in different sections. To avoid too much repetition we have also sometimes cross-referenced between chapters. Either technique is irritating if carried out to excess, so we have tried to strike a reasonable balance.

Part II

Getting started

Chapter 2

The Database wizard – or not

Access, like other Microsoft products, uses wizards to simplify and speed up commonly performed tasks. Wizards are an excellent way to learn how to complete a new task but they're not only there to help novices. Professional developers will often use wizards when appropriate, because they are the fastest way to achieve a basic end result. So, for example, I typically use the Form wizard to create a form because it does most of the ground work for me and then use the designer to modify it and make the changes I want. On the other hand, I usually build queries from scratch without the query wizard because queries are so easy to build. The bottom line is that you shouldn't feel the need to apologize for using a wizard if someone catches you doing it. I get paid for developing Access applications and use wizards whenever I think that doing so will save me time.

Access provides a set of Database wizards which can be used to generate complete, working database applications. Since you are, presumably, reading this book because you want to be able to create complete, working database applications, it seems totally perverse not to start by showing you those wizards – but that's what we are going to do. We think these wizards are great and heartily recommend that you have a look at them and see what they can do. The only problem with using them lies, not in the wizards themselves, but in the diversity of databases. No matter how many questions a wizard asks you, it cannot really be expected to generate exactly the database you need. Just like the wizards for other tasks in Access, the best it can usually do is to generate a sort of 'first approximation' to what you want. That's fine, but it means that ultimately you are still going to need to know how to use the rest of Access in order to fine tune it. So we'll leave you to play with these wizards at your leisure and get started straight away with the 'rest' of Access.

In the next chapter we'll get you to start building a database but in order to familiarize yourself with the components in Access we recommend that you start with one that already exists. We have included one on the CD-ROM called `chap2.mdb`. This is a database of names and addresses, a computerized address book if you like, which seems a reasonable place to start. The file is located in the `AccSamp` folder (see Chapter 1). Locate that file in Windows Explorer, double click on it, and Access should launch and load the database.

The database window

This is what you should see: it's the database window for the `Addresses` database. It shows you all the various components of the database and lets you reach them.

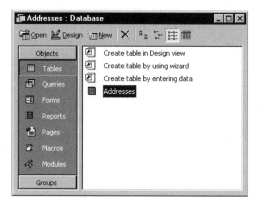

The window has two gray 'buttons' on the left-hand side labeled Objects and Groups. In the screen shot above the Objects button has been clicked so that it shows seven tabs down the left hand side – Tables, Queries etc. Each of these relates to a type of object in Access.

❢ *The computing world seems to have adopted the word 'object' as its own; the word sounds so wonderfully decisive and exact. In some areas of computing, particularly programming, the word does have a precise meaning. However, we are using it to mean 'thing', but we dare not use that word for fear of sounding too lax and unprofessional.* ❢

The first four object types (reading from top to bottom) are the four main components of a database:

- Tables
- Queries
- Forms
- Reports

In the screen shot above, the Tables tab is active.

❦ *For most of this book we'll concentrate on these four. It may now be that your curiosity is enflamed as to what the other three do; if so, flick to Chapter 21 for a very brief explanation.* ❧

We'll illustrate each of the top four components using the address book database, starting with tables.

Tables – the fundamental building blocks

Click the first tab, Tables, if it isn't already active. At the top are three options with an Access key symbol.

These identify various actions that you can perform from here, all concerned with creating new tables. We'll ignore these for the moment.

Below this is a symbol that indicates a table.

There's one of these, called `Addresses`.

Highlight the `Addresses` table and click Open, or double click on the table name. This is what you'll see.

The data in the `Addresses` table is set out in a grid, a method of displaying information clearly that's commonly used for sports scores, exchange rates, whatever. This view of a table can be referred to as the Datasheet view.

Databases are all about storing data and tables are the basic containers that all databases use for holding data. The data in a table can be presented to us in a variety of ways but when you look directly at the data in a table it is typically presented like this, as a grid of intersecting rows and columns. All areas of expertise have their own terminology and databases are no exception, so you will find in practice that rows of data are also referred to as 'records' and that columns of data are also called 'fields'.

Records and fields

Record and field are important database terms.

A record, in the context of an address database, is all the information you've gathered about where one person lives. A record comprises all the data about one entry in a table. If you had a sales database, each record would be likely to contain information about a single sales transaction.

A field equates to each piece of information you store in your database: surnames, first names, phone numbers and so on. Each of these distinct types of information is stored in a separate field.

There'll be more on fields and records in Chapter 3.

You can navigate through the data shown here in several ways. Firstly you can move the cursor around the data in the table either with the mouse or with the cursor keys. (You can also use the navigation tools at the bottom of the window but we'll illustrate these in just a moment).

❧ *The title bar that heads every Access window and dialog box can be a useful clue to what you're looking at. The bar in the previous screen shot says 'Addresses: Table', identifying the object type (Table) and giving its name (Addresses).* ❧

In practice, people mostly view the data in a database with a form (see below) but occasionally looking at the table as we have done here helps give an overview of the data.

Click the Close button to return to the database window.

Forms – and their function

Click on the Forms tab (we've skipped the Queries tab but we'll be back) where there is one form called Addresses. This is the icon that identifies a form:

Double click on Addresses and you'll see this.

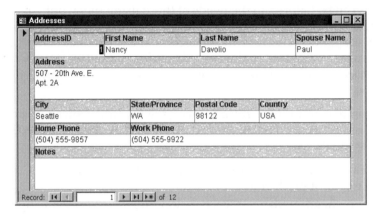

This is a form: it looks similar to the many paper forms that cross our paths. Forms are the main method of letting users interact with the data. They usually present the data in a more user-friendly fashion than the table view. Forms can also be attractive to look at, a factor which is surprisingly non-trivial. Users are almost invariably happier to interact with a database through well-designed forms that look good and have their components set out neatly and clearly. Good form design can make users more efficient and give greater satisfaction. If that doesn't convince you that form design is important – remember that happy users are more likely to generate re-peat business for database designers...

You can build many forms for a single database, indeed you can build many forms for any given table within a database. Why would you want to do that? Well, for a start, any given form doesn't have to show all the fields in a database. If you wanted to scan a table to find a contact's fax number, you could use a form which showed just the people's names and fax num-bers. This would allow you to concentrate on the job without the distrac-tion of the other fields. Another reason might be that in a business application, personnel staff could use a form showing all of an employee's data except medical records and the medical officer's form would show just the medical records. Other employees could use a form showing limited information, like phone number at work and email address. It is also possible to restrict access to these forms so that only the medical officer can see the form that shows the medical data.

Furthermore, a form can be based upon a query: the query will sort out a subset of the information stored in the database and a form based upon that query will provide user-friendly access to that information. The user of the form is thus saved from having to expend energy looking through irrelevant data.

So forms can be tailored to the needs of those using them, both in terms of content and of style. There can be data entry forms, forms for editing data and for simply displaying it. In some companies, telesales staff might appreciate a jazzier style than the executive officers. *Not that we wish to imply, for even a second, that EOs are boring (after all, they are also concerned with the repeat business process...)*

You can move around the records using the controls which appear at the bottom of all Access database forms. The small buttons show VCR-type control symbols.

- The single arrowheads move you one record at a time backwards and forwards through the database.
- The arrowheads with a vertical bar alongside take you to the first or last record in the database.
- The arrowhead with an asterisk alongside takes you to a new blank record where you can enter a new set of details.
- The box sandwiched between these controls shows you the number of the current record.
- Just to the right of these controls is the total number of records in the database.

Try moving through records one by one using these controls (it won't take you long as there are only twelve records in the sample data) and then jump back to the beginning. You can also move around the form's fields with the arrow keys on your keyboard. The Tab key works too: it steps through the fields and, on reaching the last field in a record, it moves to the first field of the next record.

Queries – questions, questions, questions...

A query is, as the name suggests, a question that you ask of your database. When you 'run' the query, Access searches for the data you have requested and presents it to you in a table. We have built a query called `LondonDetails` that looks for records in the table that relate to people who live in London. The query has also been designed only to supply the data from four of the 12 fields in the table.

Click the Close button to leave the form and click the Queries tab back in the database window and double click on LondonDetails. Queries are identified by an icon looking like this:

The answer appears in what is, with perfect logic, called an answer table.

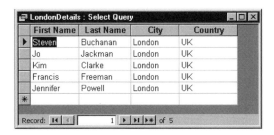

Think of a query as being a stored question. The very act of double clicking it sets the question in motion and what you see is the result, or the answer, that the query has found. The reason we suggest that you always think of queries in this way (as a question rather than as a fixed answer) is simple. If you change the data in the table and then re-run the query, you will get a different answer table (assuming that you have, in this case, added a person who lives in London).

Queries are amazingly, mind-bogglingly useful. They take the raw data in a database and turn it into hard information. They're not only for locating information in the database but also for discovering trends in the data. A query can find all the sales of yellow telephones made over the last six months. Indeed, if it was more helpful for you, the query could be constructed to show you the sales per month for the last six months so that you could see if sales are booming or fading.

Reports – printed output from a database

Click on the Reports tab to see what reports the Addresses database contains. Double click on the report called AddressesByLastName. It has an icon like this:

and the report looks like this:

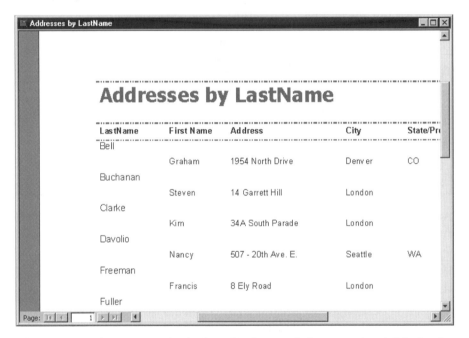

This is a simple report (of which only the top left corner is visible in the screen shot above) that lists all contacts in the database, stacked in alphabetical order. Alphabetical lists of club members, employees, customers or items for sale are used in almost every home and business.

A report is a collection of information, often summarized information, that's ready to be printed out. There are many occasions when printed output is necessary; when presenting a membership list to the club secretary, or the month's sales figures to a committee, for instance.

Reports can include all or part of each record in the database, but they really come into their own when used with queries. A report, just like a form, can be based upon a query: the query sorts out the subset of data and the report presents it. A well-designed report is easy to read, contains no super-fluous material and provides a take-home message that is abundantly clear. A badly designed one, of course, does none of the above, which is why good design is important. Reports can also contain totals, subtotals and other values generated from the data such as means, averages and percentages. Finally, reports can also be used to 'group' information. For example, suppose you want to print out a membership list from a club. You might want this grouped by region – all of the members from Arlington, followed by all those from Burlington and so on. Of course, you want them arranged alphabetically within each group, you want a sub-total after each group showing the number of members in that region and a grand total at the end. Fine, no problem; a report will do all this for you.

A brief summary of the big four

Component	Function
Table	Stores the data
Form	Provides useful views of the data
Query	Sorts out the pieces of data you want at any one time
Report	Presents data for general consumption as printed output

An understanding of these four components underpins the flexibility of Access, and in the next chapter we'll look at each in more detail.

The remaining three tabs (Pages, Macros and Modules), as we've said, we'll leave till Chapter 21 where they're introduced only briefly because none of them are required in the early stages of learning about Access.

Chapter 3

Tables – for storing your data

In Chapter 2, we looked at a ready-made database containing some data as a brief introduction to the four major components of Access – Tables, Queries, Forms and Reports. In this and the subsequent three chapters we'll cover these four components (one per chapter) using the various wizards to construct an example, while Chapter 7 is a brief refresher of the content covered thus far.

Tables are the most basic building blocks in a database; they are the containers for the data. Tables underlie all the other components and all the functionality that Access offers; the tables hold the data and the other three components (forms, queries and reports) are tools for accessing, extracting and presenting the data held in the containers.

There are two easy ways to create a table in Access 2000: one is to use the Table wizard and the other to simply start typing in your data. Here we will use the wizard because, as we've said, they are a very easy way of getting started.

Our example table will store a list of the members of a club and will, in fact, be very similar to the table in the `Addresses` database that you've already seen.

Using the Table wizard

For practice, even if Access is running, shut it down and then re-open it using the Start menu. If a dialog opens up, click the top option 'Create a new database using: Blank Access database' and then click OK. (If a dialog doesn't open up, click on File on the left of the menu bar and on New. Under the General tab, double click on Database.) In the gray panel at the top of the File New Database dialog are the words 'Save in:'. Navigate to the folder in which you want to store your sample databases. In the bottom of the dialog Access is suggesting a file name. Type in something memorable, reflecting the content of your database: my file is called `Club`. The default file type is Microsoft Access Databases (*.mdb) which is perfect.

Click the Create button to proceed.

Building a table with the Table wizard

The database window opens, giving an overview of the contents of the database: this view should already be reasonably familiar and will become more so as your learn your way around Access.

In the Objects list, the Tables button is selected. In the contents pane to the right is a list of possible actions. We'll try the middle option first: double click on 'Create table by using wizard'. This is the first page of the wizard.

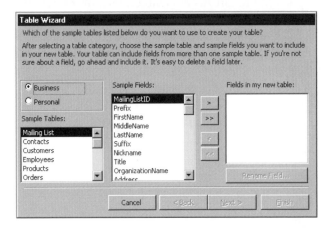

Here you define the fields in your table. First look at the panel to the left with option buttons labeled Business and Personal. Clicking on each reveals a list of ready-made Sample Tables from which to choose. Highlighting one of these Sample Tables shows a further list of the Sample Fields within the selected table. This example will be a table to store details of the members of a gardening club (well, why not?) and the Addresses table from the Personal list seems suitable.

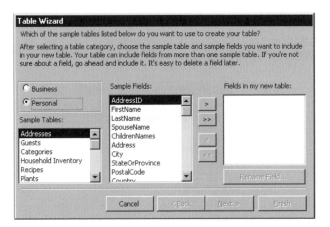

You aren't obliged to use all the fields in the list. You choose the ones you want with the selection buttons that lie between the sample fields list and the right hand list labeled 'Fields in my new table'. Highlight the

`AddressID` field, for instance, and click the top button. This transfers the selected field to your new list.

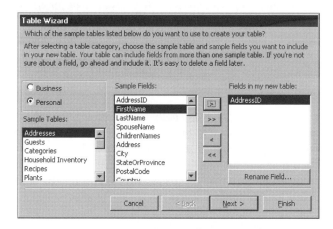

Repeat this to build up a list of all the fields you want.

❧ *Selection buttons like these occur in various dialogs. The arrowheads on the buttons indicate the direction of transfer, letting you add or remove selections from the list you're compiling. The double arrowhead buttons add or remove the whole list.* ❧

I've chosen a mere nine fields – `AddressID`, `FirstName`, `LastName`, `Address`, `City`, `PostalCode`, `EmailAddress`, `HomePhone` and `WorkPhone`. I'm using the UK localized version of Access; yours may show slightly different names here so just choose whichever seem appropriate.

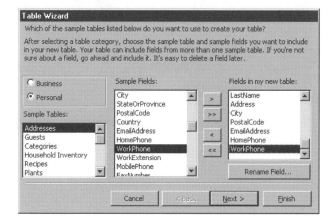

❧ *Addresses are typically split up into multiple fields, as in this case where three are used to store the information instead of storing it in a single field. Benefits accrue when you need to locate records because it will be easy to look for all those in Boston or those with 8 in the postal code.* ❧

You can edit a field name by highlighting an existing name in the 'Fields in my new table' column, clicking the Rename Field... button, typing in the new name and choosing OK.

❧ *It's good practice to choose names for your fields which reflect the content accurately. Localizing goes down well with users too; users in the States don't want to know about 'post codes' and British users balk at 'zip codes'.* ❧

Brevity is also often an advantage; for example, you might want to change the long-winded EmailAddress to Email.

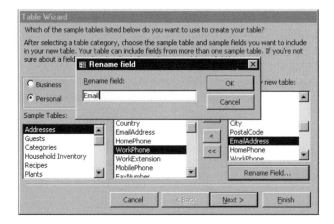

Now click the Next button.

Here you give the table a name; `ClubMembers` seems appropriate. This dialog also introduces primary key fields. At this point, let the wizard do the work, clicking the 'Yes, set a primary key for me' button.

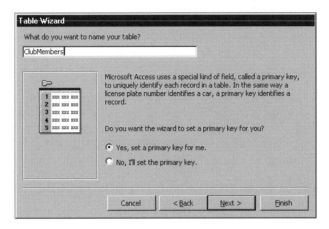

❝ *Primary keys are very important in a relational database; every table should have a primary key because they are the main way of ensuring the data entered into a table is correct and that all your future questions can be answered quickly and accurately. As to how they achieve this impressive ideal – we'll look at that in Chapter 15.* ❞

Click Next. The wizard wants to know your next move; unfortunately there's no option for 'I haven't decided what to do next, so just close the wizard' so click on the middle option so that you can see the table view of the finished table. Click on Finish and you should see a table looking like this:

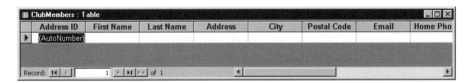

Close the wizard-created table by clicking the Close button. Back in the database window you'll see the new `ClubMembers` table in the list.

Herein a brief digression on postal code and phone number problems

Storing certain kinds of data in databases is challenging. (We don't have problems, we have challenges). We look at a way of dealing with these challenges in the section on input masks in Chapter 8, which makes it perfectly reasonable for you to ask 'Why have you bothered to bring it up now?'

The answer is that both postal codes and telephone numbers fall into the 'challenging data' category which is a shame because we often want to store precisely those pieces of information about people.

For a start, in countries like the UK, post codes (the UK specific form of a postal code) and telephone numbers don't conform to a standard format. For example, DD1 4HN and W1A 4HG are both acceptable post codes but have different formats. The former is 2 characters, 1 number, space, 1 number, 2 characters – the latter is 1 character, 1 number, 1 character, space, 1 number, 2 characters.

Even if you live in the US where formats are more controlled, we are now part of a global economy, so some/many of your contacts may be in countries other than your own. And if we leave the table as the wizard created it, you may well find that the table will reject some of the (perfectly valid) postal codes and phone numbers that you try to enter, particularly if you try to enter international ones. The good news is that it is easy to remove this restriction: all you have to do is to remove the input masks that the wizard has created for these fields.

Removing the postal code input mask

Highlight the `ClubMembers` table and then click on the Design button (second in from the left in the database window). Click on the `PostalCode` field in the list of fields in the top part of the screen. In the lower part is a list of properties on the General tab. Highlight the entry for Input Mask

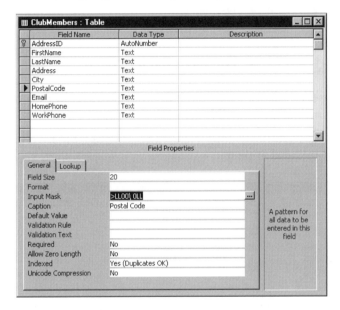

and delete it. Do the same for the `HomePhone` and `WorkPhone` input masks. Close the table with the Close button and answer Yes when asked if you want to save your changes.

This is a quick fix enabling you to work with international postal codes and phone numbers: as we said above, input masks are covered in more detail in Chapter 8.

Tables can and should be different for different kinds of data

❛ *As an aside, all the data in a table should refer to objects (things) that are similar: a table cataloging your Greek urn collection, for example, should contain Greek urn information only. So, suppose that you collect both Greek urns and books and you decide to catalog both collections in a database. If you try to store information about urns and books in the same table it will be a mess. Why? Well, you may want a field called 'Publisher' in the books table – Greek urns do not have publishers. So, don't build one table to store information about two kinds of your possessions, use two tables – one for each type (or Class) of object.* ❜

Building a table by entering data

To illustrate the other quick method of building tables, let's construct a table for that mythical *(or possibly mythological)* Greek urn collection.

In the database window, double click the 'Create table by entering data' option. A blank grid appears.

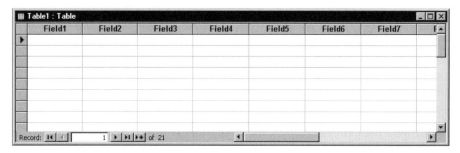

Each column has a heading, starting with `Field1` and ending with `Field10`. (More fields can be added if required.) The column headings you choose will, when the table is finished, be the fields that comprise the table.

The columns could contain information on when and where the urn was bought, its style, color and type of decoration, its dimensions, its age and a field for any additional notes. Add a name to the first column by double clicking in the gray cell that currently says `Field1`. This designation will be highlighted and you can type in your own entry. Do this for a few fields and then enter some data in the white cells below.

Height	MaxWidth	BaseColor	DesignColor	DesignType	Field6
28	18	Orange	Black	Key border and	
20	14	Ochre			

Table1 : Table

❦ *You can, in fact, type in the data and add the headings later, but this might lead to confusion if, without headings to guide you, height data was entered accidentally into the column for width data and vice versa. Suddenly your tall elegant urns are all short and squat which will earn you a poor reputation...* ❦

If you need to delete a column, click with the right mouse button in the title cell and choose Delete Column. (You don't need to delete any spare fields you don't use because only the columns that contain data will be saved as part of the table definition).

To add further columns, right click in the same way to highlight the column to the right of the position for the new column and select Insert Column. (If you add a column after you've renamed the first column, the new one appears as `Field1`.)

When you click the Close button on your new table, Access will ask if you want to save changes so answer Yes and type in a name. Access reports that no primary key field has been chosen for the table so click the Yes button to let Access add a suitable field.

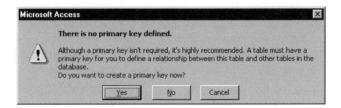

Microsoft Access

There is no primary key defined.

Although a primary key isn't required, it's highly recommended. A table must have a primary key for you to define a relationship between this table and other tables in the database.
Do you want to create a primary key now?

Yes   No   Cancel

This is how the Datasheet view of the `Urns` table should look with a few more records added. The first field, labeled `ID`, is the one Access added to act as the primary key field.

ID	Height	MaxWidth	BaseColor	DesignColor	DesignType
1	28	18	Orange	Black	Key border and figures
2	20	14	Ochre	Black	Key border
3	15	14	Ochre	Dark crimson	Fruit & flowers
4	15	14	Ochre	Dark crimson	Vegetables & flowers
5	17	9	Terracotta	Black	Key border
6	14	9	Chestnut	Black	Figures
7	12	12	Ochre	Black	Key border & figures
8	14	10	Terracotta	Black	Flowers
(AutoNumber)					

Record: 1 of 8

Adding records

When you start typing data into a table, a pencil icon appears in the gray square to the far left of the row. This indicates that the record has been altered but not yet saved, or 'posted', in database terminology. Moving down to the next row automatically posts an entry, as does clicking on the pencil icon.

What do we mean by 'posting' the entry? Well, when you use a word processor to create a letter, you save the letter at intervals as you work, or you set the word processor to do it for you, or you live dangerously and only save the finished letter. Access sometimes works in the same way. For example, when you create and edit a form, it exists only in the memory of the machine until you actively save that form. If the machine crashes, the form will be lost. The same is true for reports and queries and even when you are creating a table. However, once a table has been created and you start entering data, Access treats the data in a table very differently. Every record that you create and/or edit is treated as a valuable entity. As soon as you move to another record, the one upon which you have been working is saved to disk. The good news is that the data in your database is much more likely to survive if your machine has a problem. The bad news is that you cannot undo multiple edits to multiple records. Some undo ability is allowed via the interface, and the general rules are as follows:

- If you are editing a record and you haven't moved off that record, you can undo any and all changes using the Esc key.

- If you change record A, post those changes and start to edit record B, you can undo the changes to B using Esc and undo the changes to A using the Undo button in the button bar.

But that's it. You can't undo earlier changes that you have made to other records and although these general rules apply most of the time, in certain Access applications you may not be able to undo any changes. So the bottom line is, be careful out there when you're dealing with important data. It is well worth playing around with a table of test data to get a feel for what you can and can't do before working with real data.

Field names

If you skipped Chapter 1, we strongly recommend that, at this point, you read the section called 'What's in a name?' The advice given there can safely be ignored for this first table but is worth following for real databases that you build in the future.

Records and fields revisited

A record comprises all the data you collect for one person, urn or whatever. In the address book example, everything entered in the database about Person X comprises their record – which is a single row in the table.

Records are made up of fields and the fields reflect the individual pieces of information being collected. The address table has fields for first name, last name, phone number and so on – each field is a column in the table.

❛ *The terms 'row' and 'record' are often used more or less interchangeably, as are 'field' and 'column'. If you want some guidance, as a general rule, if I was talking about the table structure itself, I would tend to talk about rows and columns ('This table has 5 columns and 20 rows.') If I was talking about the data I would tend to use field and record ('The* `LastName` *field in John's record contains the value "Parker".') But this is not a hard and fast rule – only a pedant would differentiate too forcefully.* ❜

Address ID	First Name	Last Name	Address	City	Postal Code	Email	Home Phone
1	Simon	Jackson	1234 Lime Tree Drive	Carmel	94652	sj@email	123-456-7890
2	Maria	Carlson	34 Minton Road	London	SW4 2HJ		0181 234 5678
3	Paula	Andrews	17 George Street	London	W4 3JK	paula@email	0171 444 4444
4	David	Hassall	143 Western Way	Tacoma	98467	dh@email	987-654-3210
5	Gordon	Grant	128 Lothian Road	Edinburgh	EH1 1RD	gordong@email	
6	Felicia	Sharmain	2453 Rose Bvd	San Francisco	94117	fee@email	111-222-3333

If you've worked through the chapter thus you should have a database like the one in the file called `chap3.mdb`.

The screen shot above shows the `ClubMembers` table from the `Club` database just as described above but with some data added. We use this table and this data in Chapter 4.

Queries – finding data

Why you need to use queries

Creating and maintaining databases is fun (or at least I find it so) but ultimately we don't do all this work for the fun of it, we do it because sometime, somewhere, we are going to want to get data back out of the database. Typically we use queries to do this for us.

What is a query?

Queries can be simple: 'How many contacts do I have in Fontana or Frankfurt?', for instance, or more complex: 'Do I know anyone with a birthday in May who uses AOL as a service provider and lives in Oregon?' Given a business application, even more complex queries can be imagined: 'What are last year's sales figures, month by month, for each sales representative working in Europe but ignoring sales of the new product SuperClean?'

Queries can be saved for future use. You can build queries for questions that are asked regularly about the data. For example, you could construct a query which lists the current membership of a club or another which works out the turnover for the current month. When a need arises for up-to-date information, simply run the saved query and it will produce the current answer.

The answer to a query appears in a table or, more specifically, in an answer table. This has the look and feel of a table, but it does not, in fact, have any lasting existence and you won't find it listed in the Tables tab of the current database window. An answer table is a 'virtual' table; as soon as you close the query, the answer table ceases to exist. In case this sounds like a problem, it isn't. Typically you don't want an answer table to be permanent (and if you ever do, as explained later, Access provides an easy way for you to achieve this) and the default therefore is for transitory answer tables.

Using the Query wizard

The easiest way to build a query is (you've probably guessed) to let a wizard do it.

Building a query

Load the `Club` database (`chap4start.mdb`) from the `AccSamp` folder: this is the same database as the one constructed by the end of Chapter 3 except that it has data in it. In the database window, click on the Queries tab. There are two options for creating queries: choose the wizard method with a double click. (You can see a greater selection of query wizards by clicking the New button from the database window menu. If you elect to do it this way, choose the Simple Query Wizard for now).

Here you select the table and fields to use in the query using essentially the same methods as in the Table wizard. Select the `ClubMembers` table from the pop down list of Tables/Queries and then inspect the list of Available Fields below.

For this example I'll include, say, the `FirstName`, `LastName` and `City` fields.

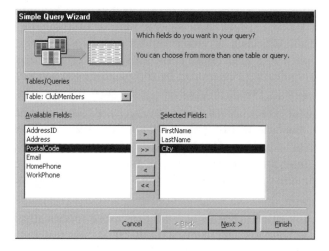

Now click the Next button, give your query a name (I've used `People`) and click Finish to accept the default 'Open the query to view information'.

❛ *As a general rule it is worth picking memorable and informative names for the objects that you create in Access. I realize that 'People' doesn't follow this rule but the query is so simple that a choosing a meaningful name represents something of a challenge!* ❜

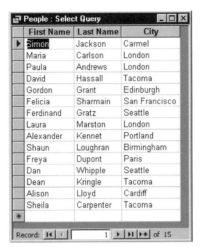

Here's the result of your query. The title bar reads People: Select Query. Your query has 'selected' a set of records corresponding to the responses you gave the wizard. In this case, the set selected comprises data from three of the fields and all of the records in the table.

This wizard, like its name says, builds only simple queries. You can choose a subset of fields but you cannot specify a subset of records. This is a limitation because the majority of questions asked of a database demand a subset of both fields and records: the names of my contacts based in London or Long Beach, the prices of the silk shirts or all the addresses from the July invoices.

The other query building wizards – 'Crosstab', 'Find Duplicates' and 'Find Unmatched' – all tend to be relatively specialized. In practice, the only way to create a simple query that subsets both the records and fields is to use the Query Design tool. However, the good news, as I implied in Chapter 2, the query design tool is so easy to use that I rarely use the query wizards. With that in mind we'll move on rapidly.

The Query Design tool

With the Query Design tool you can build anything from the simplest to all but the most complex queries.

Creating a simple query

Close the `People` answer table and back in the database window, click 'Create query in Design view'.

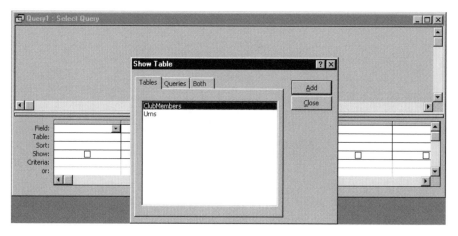

This pops up the Show Table dialog with a window behind it. The active dialog has three tabs: our query will be based on the `ClubMembers` table again so from the Tables tab, double click it. A representation of the chosen table now appears in the background window.

That's all we need but if you look in the Queries tab, you'll see your People query. *(If you are now beginning to wonder whether this means that you can perform the recursive-sounding process of basing queries on other queries, you're right. We have a look at that in Chapter 9).* And if you look in the Both tab – well, you guess.

Your actions so far have determined the table upon which the query is to be built and placed it in the Query Design window. When you click Close in the Show Table dialog, you see this:

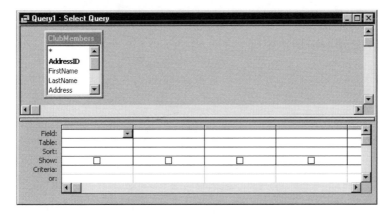

There are two main elements to the Query Design window:

The top section is the Table/Query pane and shows the table(s) on which the new query is based.

Beneath that is the Query Design pane, a grid where you define the query. Each column of the grid can contain one field and the information which narrows the search for data in that field.

Finding the right fields

The first step in building any query is to select fields to appear in the query answer.

In the table in the upper pane, the top row contains just an asterisk (*); this is formally known as the 'all fields reference tag'. This is Access-speak for 'include all fields in the query'. Double click on it and the field name `ClubMembers.*` appears in the Field row of the grid.

❻ *To identify a field unequivocally in Access, it's written as `TableName. FieldName`. The entry in the field row of the query grid is `ClubMembers.*`, meaning all fields in the `ClubMembers` table.* ❾

The table name in shown the Table row and the check box in the Show row is checked.

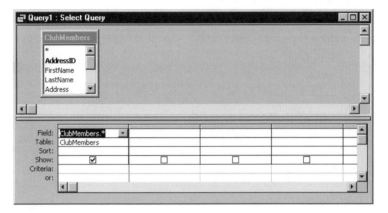

If this check box is checked, the field will be visible in the completed query.

❻ *The last statement may sound odd and could reasonably provoke the question 'Why would I ever select a field that I **don't** want to see in the answer?' Well, for example, suppose you want to find every member in Seattle. You will need the City field to be included in the query in order to select those members. But it is pointless to make the City field visible in the answer table because every record will contain the same value – Seattle. 'Ah, but', you argue 'I **want** it to be visible in order to check that my query is working properly.' OK, that's fine, the choice is yours and I often do the same, particularly when I first create a query. But once you are happy that the query is working properly, you may well find it useful, particularly when working with big sets of data, to be able to remove the field.* ❾

The query looks like an exercise in minimalism but run it anyway by either clicking on the Run button:

or on the View button

which flips you between the Design view (where you define the query) and the Datasheet view (where you can see the results).

For now these two buttons appear to do exactly the same job i.e. let you see the answer. They do have subtly different functions and all will be revealed in Chapter 9.

Despite the minimalist query, all the fields in the table have been selected and the data from each is displayed.

Address ID	First Name	Last Name	Address	City	Postal Code	Email	Ho
1	Simon	Jackson	1234 Lime Tree Drive	Carmel	94652	sj@email	123
2	Maria	Carlson	34 Minton Road	London	SW4 2HJ		018
3	Paula	Andrews	17 George Street	London	W4 3JK	paula@email	017
4	David	Hassall	143 Western Way	Tacoma	98467	dh@email	333
5	Gordon	Grant	128 Lothian Road	Edinburgh	EH1 1RD	gordong@email	
6	Felicia	Sharmain	2453 Rose Bvd	San Francisco	94117	fee@email	111
7	Ferdinand	Gratz	1003 Shore Road	Seattle	98128		222
8	Laura	Marston	17a Walton Road	London	E11 5HN		018
9	Alexander	Kennet	123 Ridgeway Road	Portland	97219	alexk@email	
10	Shaun	Loughran	12 South Parade	Birmingham	B5 3GH		012
11	Freya	Dupont	12 Rue de Soleil	Paris	75627	freya_dupont@e	
12	Dan	Whipple	2073 Hill Street	Seattle	98345	daniel@email	222
13	Dean	Kringle	1863 Bridge Bvd	Tacoma	98451	kringle2@email	333
14	Alison	Lloyd	178 Bridge Street	Cardiff	CF4 5WL	a_lloyd@email	
15	Sheila	Carpenter	144 Sunset Road	Tacoma	98463		333
* (AutoNumber)							

Record: ⏮ ◀ 1 ▶ ⏭ ▶* of 15

Making use of an asterisk in a query is a very quick way of building a query that shows all of the fields in the table. Using the Query Design tool you could get the same result by picking each field manually but the asterisk method brings other advantages apart from speed. If you save such a query, the results will always include all fields, even if you've deleted fields from the table or added new ones since you last ran the query.

Close the answer table by clicking the Close button. Access asks if you want to save the new query (provisionally entitled Query1). We might as well save it as the informatively named AllInfo.

Now let's create a query from a limited set of fields.

Start as before, selecting the `ClubMembers` table for use in the query grid.

To include a subset of fields in a query, add them one at a time. Double click on the `FirstName` field from the `ClubMembers` table in the upper pane. This puts the field name into the Field row of the grid, the table name into Table row, and a check into the Show row.

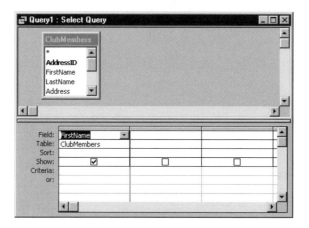

Repeat to select all required fields: I'm using `FirstName`, `LastName` and `City`.

Run the query.

Now a subset of fields is displayed for all records.

Incidentally, I'd love to tell you that I was good enough to always build exactly the query I want first time, but it isn't true for me and I suspect it isn't for most database designers. Designing a query is often an iterative process. You do some of the design work, run the query and see what you get, alter the design a bit, run it again and so on until it is perfect. So, for example, in this case, perhaps you want to see phone numbers as well. To swop back into the Design view, click the View button, which now looks like this:

Back in design mode, you can modify the query by adding or removing further fields.

Now you can create queries using all fields or just some of them, what about controlling which of the records will appear in the answer table?

Finding the right records

We'll continue to work with the current query so return to the Design view. A glance at the Query Design grid shows that there is a row labeled Criteria (and one labeled, mysteriously, 'or') and this is where you determine the records to be displayed.

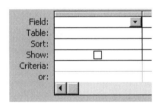

The entry you make in the Criteria row is the information that Access will try to find in that field, so on the Criteria row in the `City` column, type:

    seattle

This says, in English, 'select the record only if the entry in the city field says Seattle'.

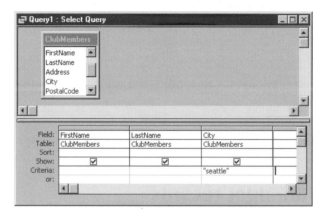

❛ *When you type 'seattle' as a criterion and then move the cursor (say by pressing the tab key), Access automatically wraps the word in quotes so you don't have to bother – another time-saving device brought to you by Access. The match also happens to be case-insensitive so it will find 'seattle', 'Seattle', 'seAttlE' etc.* ❜

Run the query and see if your result looks like this:

There should be two people living in Seattle, Ferdinand Gratz and Dan Whipple, and that's your first answer comprising a subset of records.

Return to the design view. On the 'or' row in the City column, type:

london

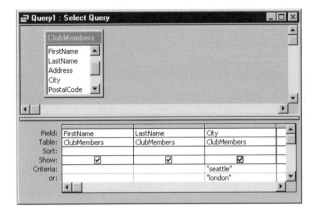

Run the query and you should see this:

It shouldn't be a surprise that the Seattle residents' records have been joined by those of some Londoners. The English rendition of the criteria is now 'select the record if the entry in the city field says either Seattle or London'.

❦ *And by the way, suppose you want these records sorted alphabetically by last name. Simply flip back to design mode and select 'Ascending' in the Sort option underneath* `LastName`.

Further criteria can be added in subsequent rows.

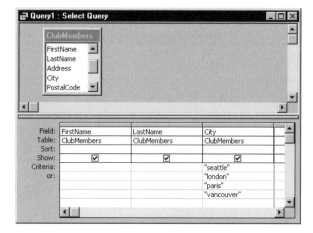

You're not limited to setting criteria for a single field, however. If you want the records for anyone living in London whose name is Laura, the criteria in the City column would read 'london' and in the FirstName column, 'laura'. Criteria in different columns are taken to be joined with an 'and': in English the query says 'show me the records where the city field contains 'london' and where the first name field contains 'laura'.

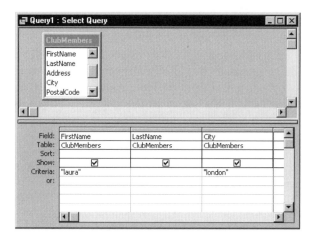

> *The results of expressions containing 'and' and 'or' can sometimes cause confusion. If you use 'or' you will, as a general rule, get a larger answer set than if you use 'and'. At first glance, this may seem odd. What the 'or' is saying is 'Accept a record for display in the answer table if it contain either x **or** y, so you get all the records which contain x and all those that contain y. 'And' says 'Accept only those records that contain both x **and** y' so you only get the records that meet both criteria.*

Operators

'and' and 'or' are both operators. These are used in queries and also in other parts of Access. Now seems like a good time to cover them and while we are at it we'll look at wildcards.

Operators are used to modify the way in which (in this case) the criteria work. So far we have come across two operators – 'and' and 'or'. However, there are others that you can use. Remember when you typed in the word 'seattle' as a criterion, it worked fine because the `City` field contains text information and we wanted an exact match to the word. Suppose that you were using the `Urns` table and wanted to find all of the urns shorter than 20 units tall. This information is in a numeric field so you are clearly going to use '20' as the criterion. However, if you simply use '20', the answer table will simply list those urns that are exactly 20 units high. Using '<20' will do the job perfectly because '<' is an operator that means 'Less than'. The table below lists the common operators.

Commonly used operators	
Symbol	*Meaning*
*	Multiply
+	Add
-	Subtract
/	Divide
=	Equal
<	Less than
>	Greater than
<=	Less than or equal to
>=	Greater than or equal to
<>	Not equal to
Is null	Doesn't contain data

> *Null values are discussed in Chapter 8 but in essence a field that doesn't contain any data is said to be null, or to contain a null value.*

As a general rule the '=' symbol is assumed if you don't supply one; hence when you typed 'seattle', this was taken to mean '=seattle'.

Wildcards

So far, so good. But suppose that you want to find customers in Seattle but you can't remember how to spell the name of that city. Access will allow you to use what in computing are called wildcards – '*'and '?'.

'*' means substitute any number of characters here. So, assuming that you know that Seattle starts with an 'S', you could type in 'S*'. Access will turn this into 'Like "s*"'

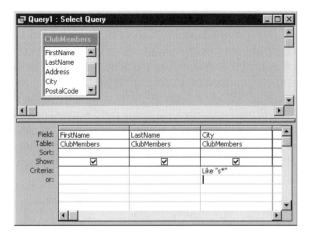

When the query runs, you find the correct records, you discover how Seattle is spelt and, as an added bonus, you also find the records for San Francisco.

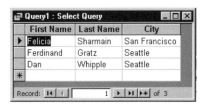

The '?' wildcard is much more specific (and therefore used less frequently) and substitutes for a single character. Thus 'car???' will find Carmel but not Cardiff (both of which exist as cities in the ClubMembers table) because Cardiff has seven letters, not six.

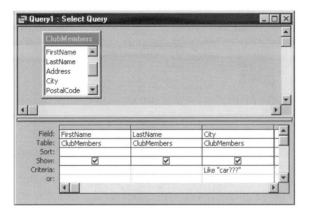

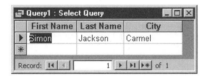

Note that when you type in a criterion such as 'car???', Access will convert this to:

  Like "car???"

This simply means 'Find the records which are like this'. Of course, you can type the expression in full, but why not let Access do the hard work?

We've been experimenting with this query and don't need to save it so, when the experiments are over, there's no need to save it though you can do so if you wish.

Finding both fields and records

The foregoing methods can be used to produce an answer which is both a subset of fields and a subset of records. This, in fact, is what most queries are and it's also what gives queries their flexibility.

To illustrate this, we'll build a query which looks for all residents of Tacoma and shows their names and phone numbers.

Start with a new query constructed from the Design view and based on the ClubMembers table. Add four fields: first and last name, city and home phone number. Type the criterion:

tacoma

into the City column and run the query. This is the answer:

Do you really need to see Tacoma listed three times in the answer? You already know you're looking for Tacoma residents; you might even have named the query TacomaResidents. Flip to the design view. Click in the Show box in the City column to remove the check and run the query again.

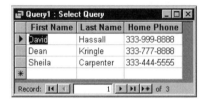

This is a good example of why it's useful to be able to include a field in a query without displaying its contents as part of the answer table.

Multiple queries per table

A query can be saved for future use and many queries can be associated with a single table. This brings efficiency gains and saves time; particularly useful queries and ones which are likely to be run often (monthly sales, for instance) can be used time and time again.

Saving queries

When a query is working correctly and you are likely to use it again, save it.

With your query on the screen (either in Design or View mode), click File, Save from the menu, or the Save button, or press Ctrl+S on the keyboard.

In the resulting Save As dialog, enter a name for your query (mine is Tacoma)

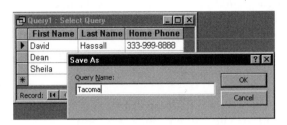

and click OK. Return to the database window and the new query should be listed under the Queries tab.

When you want to run the new query, activate the Query tab of the database window and double click on the query. It will run and generate an up-to-date answer from the data in your database.

Saving data with a make-table query

Not only can you save the query, you can save the result it generates too. Mostly it's enough to save a query for future use so that you generate an up-to-date answer each time you run it. Occasionally, however, it is useful to have a snapshot of the answer returned at a particular time.

To turn the answer table produced by a query into a new table in the database, you use a Make-table query.

With the Tacoma query open in Design view, look at the title bar which says Tacoma: Select Query. 'Select' simply describes the action of the query: it selects the records as per your query definition.

❻ *Queries have a terminology all of their own and much of it comes from a language specifically designed for building complex queries. The language is SQL, Structured Query Language, and 'select' is one of its commands. You're unlikely to need to know anything more about SQL as Access' graphical query tool is sufficiently powerful to make SQL unnecessary except for highly specialized querying.*

SQL, by the way, is pronounced variously as 'Ess-que-ell' and 'Sequel'; the former predominates in Britain and the latter in the US. ❾

For the current task we need a different type of query. Still in the Design view, find the Query Type icon in the top menu

and click on the arrowhead in the bar to its right. Click on Make-Table Query... from the pop down list. (If this option isn't listed, click the double arrowhead button to extend the list). In the Make Table dialog box, type a name for the new table such as `TacomaResidents` and ensure the Current Database option button is selected.

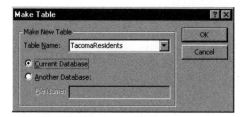

Click OK. As can be seen from the title bar, the `Tacoma` query is now a Make-Table query and it will generate a table called TacomaResidents. When you close it, Access asks if you want to save it in its new guise. Answer Yes and in the database window, its icon changes to reflect its new type.

Now try running it. Access will check two things with you: firstly, that you're aware of the query's type: click Yes to continue. Secondly, Access asks if it's OK to proceed with pasting data into a new table.

❻ *Access is ensuring that you remember that each time a Make-Table query is run, the data in the table will be over-written with the most recent results from the query.* ❾

Answer Yes again and the answer table appears. Close the table and look in the Tables tab of the database window. There's the new table which you can open and inspect just like any other table.

❦ *A table created with the Make-Table query does not inherit the primary key property nor all of the other field properties from the original table. There's more on both these topics in Chapter 8.* ❧

If you run the query a second time, Access will check three things. Firstly, as before, that you know it's a Make Table query, secondly, that the existing `TacomaResidents` table will be deleted, and thirdly that data will be pasted into a new table. One more point seems worth making here. As described above, Access overwrites the `TacomaResidents` table each time. If you want to preserve any particular copy of the table, simply rename it. You can do this by right clicking on the name of the table, selecting Rename and adding, say, a 1. When you rerun the query it will generate a new table with the name `TacomaResidents` leaving `TacomaResidents1` intact.

Summary

With queries you can pull selected information out of a database and in this chapter we've introduced that most straightforward and most useful type of query, the Select query that allows you to select exactly the information you require. Make-Table queries are rather less commonly used but can be very useful on occasions.

The database constructed so far is contained in the file `chap4end.mdb`.

Chapter 5

Forms – viewing and entering data

You are well aware that you can see data in tables so you may be wondering why forms are needed at all because they show data too. What, then, is the difference?

A table is a table is a table. It stores data and that's its primary function. Forms can be thought of as gateways into the table: you can enter data into a table via a form, use a form to view data, edit it and manipulate it. True, you can do all these things by interacting directly with the table without creating any forms at all but there is no easy way of modifying what a user sees of a table: it's all or nothing. With a form, you can restrict the visible fields so that the form acts like a filter on the data in the table. In addition, a whole range of different forms can be associated with one table. So, as we said in Chapter 2, Access allows you to restrict who can use which form (and stop people getting to the underlying table) so that nobody has to wade through irrelevant data and no-one can get to information that they shouldn't see.

Forms are also generally more helpful to the user than tables. You can label fields with terms that mean something to the user of the form, rather than hoping they'll understand the terminology used by the designer of the table. You can also put messages to the user on the screen and provide ways of making data entry less tedious and hence less likely to contain errors.

So tables are the core of a database and hold the data, but users of the database will typically interact with that data via one or more forms.

Really rapid form creation

Access has a one-click mechanism for creating forms: this speed freak is the AutoForm and we'll use it to create a form for entering new addresses into the Club database.

If you're following the examples, start with the database in chap5start.mdb. In the Tables tab of the database window, ensure that the ClubMembers table is highlighted. Click Insert on the main menu and choose AutoForm – and there's a whole new form that includes all fields.

You can also create an AutoForm by highlighting the table upon which you wish it based and clicking the down arrow alongside the New Object button

and selecting AutoForm. If hover help says New Object: AutoForm as your mouse hovers over the button, you can just click the button itself. Hover help shows the last use that was made of the New Object button.

You can save an AutoForm in the usual way: I've called it `AllFields`. To add a new record using the new form, click on the New Record button on the toolbar or on the form and you're ready to enter new data.

As discussed, this form contains all of the fields in the table; such forms are often used for data entry so that as complete a record as possible is entered. But suppose that you want to create a more specialized form which shows only some of the fields? For this you can use the Form wizard.

Using the Form wizard

In the database window, click the Forms tab and double click 'Create form by using wizard'. In the first step of the Form wizard, select the table with which to work: we'll stick with ClubMembers and build a form to view names and postal addresses.

Move the appropriate fields from the Available Fields panel to the Selected Fields panel with the arrow keys

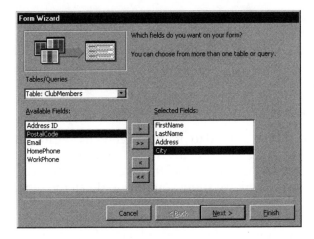

and click Next. Four layout types are offered for your form; a sample is displayed as you click on each of the four options. I've chosen the Justified layout and, in the next page, the style called Stone.

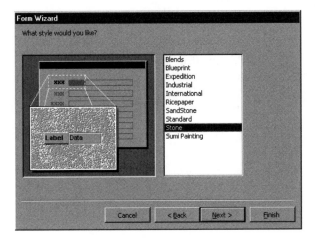

Click Next. Give the form a title (I've used `PostalAddresses`) and check that the option button for 'Open the form to view or enter information' is selected. Click Finish and you have a form for viewing name and address information from the club membership database.

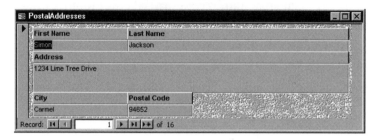

Creating different types of form

The Form wizard can be used to produce a good usable form and Access allows you to customize this form in an almost infinite series of ways. This is done with the form designer, a tool that we examine in detail in Chapters 10 and 11. That's where we show you how to do all the fun things like inserting pictures, changing colors and so on. Moderately surprisingly, we have resisted the temptation to go straight to the colorful bit and in this chapter we have concentrated on introducing the less visually stimulating but more useful topic of calculated values.

Calculated values

Suppose that you want to store information about people. If that information includes, say, pension information, you will need to know how old each person is. So should you store their age in the table? The obvious (and correct) answer is 'no' because that information would have to be updated every time each person had a birthday. However, suppose that you store each person's date of birth in the table and use a form to look at the data. As each record is displayed in the form, the current age of the person can be calculated by Access and displayed.

❧ *We won't actually demonstrate how to create this one because, despite being a great example to which most people can relate, it happens to be rather tortuous to do in practice (because the calendar we use is complex) and is best solved using the Access programming language. However, we also understand that using it as an example and not providing a solution is likely to be frustrating if an age calculation just hap-pens to be exactly what you need for your database. So we have included an example in the file called* `Chap5ages`*. Feel free to look at it if the subject interests you.*

We'll demonstrate calculated values with another example, where we can concentrate on the method rather than the intricacies of date manipula-tion. Suppose you store information about Grecian urns. Amongst the in-formation stored in the database is the height and the width of each urn. Suppose also that you frequently move the urns around and so you need to know the smallest packing case that will accommodate each urn. Your car-rier isn't interested in the shape, just the external volume of each case, in order to calculate the shipping charges. Should you also store that informa-tion in the table of information about urns? The answer is again 'no' be-cause that information is already inherently stored in the table. To calculate the external volume of the case required (assuming that the case walls and packaging are 1.5 units thick on each side) all you have to do is to multiply (height + 3) * (width + 3) * (width + 3).

We call data that is inherent in other data 'derivable' or 'redundant' data for the simple reason that it can be derived from the existing data and therefore storing it is redundant. As a pretty hard and fast rule, you shouldn't store derivable data in a table. Instead you get the computer to calculate it for you whenever you need it. This can be done using a form (as we'll demonstrate here) or using a query (as demonstrated later in Chapter 9). Since the users of your database will only view the data using a form, as far as they are concerned, the age of the person or the shipping volume of the urn is always visible. Indeed, they may believe that the information is stored in the database – that's fine; as long as the database is useful to them, it doesn't matter how the information is stored.

Forms performing calculations

Putting a calculation on a form means using the Design view but we'll start by building a simple form with the Form wizard. Based on the `Urns` table, the form uses the fields `ID`, `Height`, `MaxWidth` and `DesignType`. I've called it `TestCalc` and the finished form looks like this:

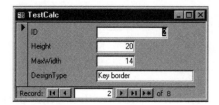

Flip into Design view by pressing the design button:

The form now looks like this:

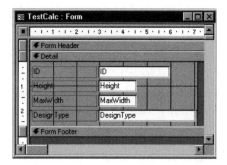

Design view gives you the tools you need for controlling how a form looks and behaves. You can move the fields around, remove them and add different ones, change the sizes, colors, fonts, patterns, borders, add text messages to the user and all sorts of other stuff that's covered in detail in Chapters 10 and 11. You can also, of course, add calculations, and we'll do that now.

I'm going to add a calculated field to this form. It will add the value 3 to each dimension and then multiply the figures together to calculate the shipping volume.

First, give yourself some more room on the form by placing the cursor on the bottom right corner of the gridded area, called the Detail section, which denotes the shape of the finished form. When the cursor shows as a four-headed arrow, drag the area out a bit.

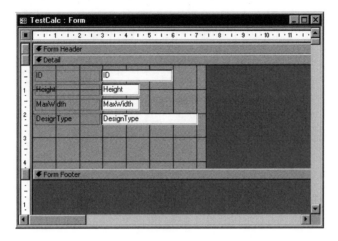

Calculations are almost always placed in text boxes on a form; check out the Toolbox

✎ *(If you can't find the toolbox, select View, Toolbox from the main menu.)* **❾**

Within the Toolbox locate the Text Box tool.

Click it and move the cursor onto the form. Click and drag to outline a text box: make your first click some way in from the left hand edge of the form so there's room for both the text box and for the accompanying label that's placed to its left. Play with the various handles to move it around and resize it: to move the label (which will say 'Text8:' or some such number) or the text box independently, put the cursor on the top left corner whereupon it changes into a hand-with-pointing-finger. (A cursor showing a spread hand moves the two together).

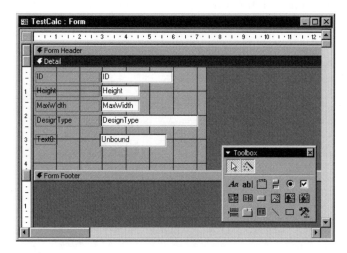

❝ *There now follows a brief digression on objects and their properties.* ❞

Objects and properties

Everything on a form is an object and every object has a set of properties. (In this case we are using the term 'object' in a slightly more formal sense than in Chapter 2). Objects are things like fields, labels, the detail, header and footer sections and the form itself. Properties are things like the size, color, font, caption and so on. Different objects have different selections of properties, just like objects in real life. For instance, a notebook would have a 'number of pages' property which has no meaning for, say, a fish.

To see the properties of any object, place the cursor on it, click the right mouse button and select Properties, last on the list. A list like this will pop out.

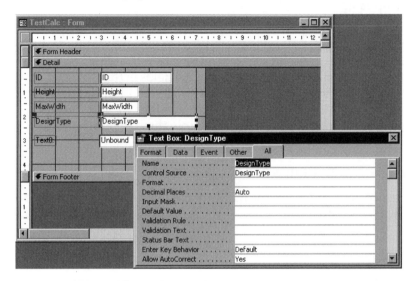

You can also see an object's properties by selecting it and clicking the Properties button.

To see the properties of the form, rather than those of the individual objects that make up the form, click on the Form Selector. This is the gray square in the top left hand corner of the form in Design view.

When you click it, a black square appears in the form selector and the properties for the whole form are now listed. Clicking on any other object returns the form selector to plain gray and changes the property list to show the properties of the object you have now selected.

For any given object there is a number of tabs in the Properties dialog – typically five: Format, Data, Event, Other and All (which combines information from the previous four). You can leave the Properties dialog open and move the cursor to another object and the properties shown in the dialog will be updated.

Inspect the Data properties of the new text box. The first property is Control Source: this tells the text box where to get the information to display on the form. Put the cursor in the Control Source cell and two buttons appear to the right. The first pops down a list of the fields in the table that underlies the form. We don't want data from a single field but the data from two (Height and MaxWidth) manipulated such that we add three to each (to allow for the packaging) and then multiply them together.

In pseudo English the equation would read something like:

(height + 3) * (width + 3) * (width + 3).

In practice, we need to use the names of the fields that hold the data so that this equation reads as:

([Height]+3)*([MaxWidth]+3)*([MaxWidth]+3)

All we have to do is to add an equals sign to the front and we get:

=([Height]+3)*([MaxWidth]+3)*([MaxWidth]+3)

which is what you need to type in as the control source

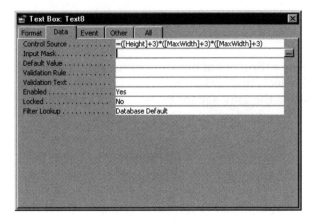

While we are here in Design mode, you could also change the Caption of the new label to something more sensible. You could also decide to hide the height and width fields so just the volume is shown on the form: in the Format properties of the Height text box, change the Visible property from Yes to No (click the arrow and choose).

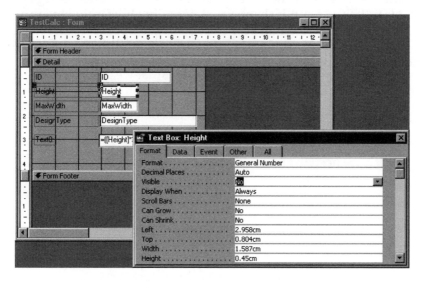

Do the same for MaxWidth and inspect the form again.

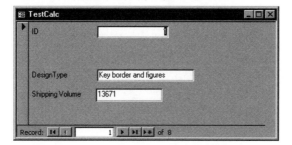

Multiple forms per table

As mentioned briefly above, many forms can be associated with one table. Creating a range of forms could simplify the performance of various tasks, making data entry more enjoyable, maintenance of existing data less confusing and so on. It also lets you give users exactly the tool they need for a particular job.

Summary

Building forms is quick and easy using the Form wizard and AutoForm while for more adventurous forms, the Form Design tool provides the needful. As we've said, there'll be a lot more about the Form Design tool in Chapters 10 and 11 as this chapter contains only a brief introduction. Using the wizard and the Design view in conjunction speeds up development time as you can start with a wizard-generated form that's almost perfect and then fine tune it with the tools in the Design view.

Chapter 6

Reports – printing your data

Demands for data in printed form continue to rise. 'Can you just run me off a copy of the latest stock levels/employee details/baseball scores?' So much for the paperless office.

Reports are Access's way of preparing data for printing, with headings, page numbers and the information arranged in helpful groups. Looking at the Report wizard will provide a good overview.

Creating a report using the Report wizard

Start with the `chap6start.mdb` file. Under the Reports tab in the `Club` database window, double click on 'Create report by using wizard'. The goal in this example is to print out a list of members, complete with phone numbers.

In the first screen, select the table on which to base the report (good old `ClubMembers`) and then choose the fields you want in the report. I've chosen all fields except the `AddressID` field.

Click the Next button. The wizard asks if you want any 'grouping levels': we'll ignore this for now (but we'll do it in Chapter 12) so click the Next button.

Here you can specify the sort order for the records. Mostly we find a person's phone number by looking up the last name, so select LastName from the pop down list in the top sort slot. Either stick with the default A–Z order or swop to Z–A order if you're feeling perverse (or perpetually hard-done-by as you would be if your last name was Whitehorn...).

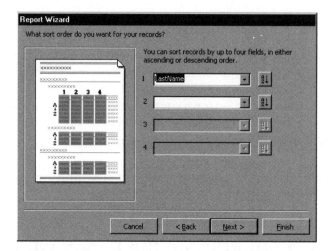

Click Next. In this dialog, the wizard offers six layouts for the report (a sample is shown when you make a selection), two paper orientations and a very handy check box for juggling things so that all the chosen fields fit on one page. My settings are Tabular layout and landscape orientation.

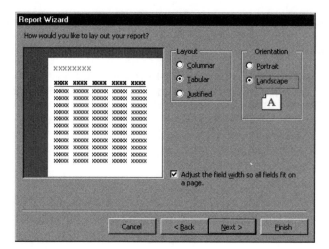

❧ *The 'Adjust the field width so all fields fit on a page' check box could also be referred to as a 'print to fit' check box. This latter name is short and apposite – it prints the output so it fits onto the page neatly.*

This option is certainly useful but it doesn't possess supernatural powers. If you have lots of fields in your portrait-orientated report all packed with long text entries, it can't possibly fit it onto a single page. Access will do its best but field names and contents are likely to appear truncated when you print out the report. ❧

Choose a layout and orientation and click Next, then choose a style and click Next. Name the report (mine is `PhoneList`) and click Finish with the 'Preview the report' option selected (the default).

This is part of the resulting report.

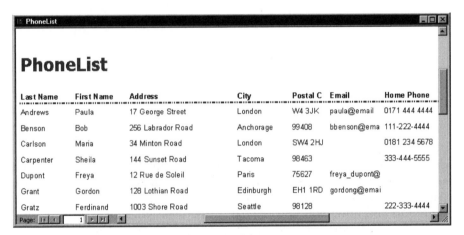

Creating other wizard-generated reports

Having already met AutoForms in Chapter 5, you might have noticed AutoReport listed under the New Object button or the Insert menu option. They'll let you generate even swifter reports than the Report wizard. You have little control over what's produced and sometimes the results are less than optimal but for all the time it takes to try, it's often worth generating one to see if it will do.

Highlight the ClubMembers table in the Tables tab, click the arrow alongside the New Object button, select AutoReport and that's it.

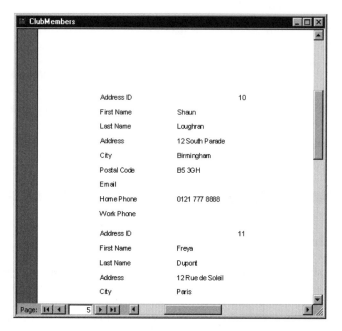

Hmm, not so great, this one. It's simply a list of entries in which it would be hard to locate a specific phone number or even person as the records are listed in the order they were entered into the ClubMembers table. Close the report and don't bother to save it. Some you win, some you lose.

Other types of AutoReport are available from the New button in the database window. With the Reports tab selected, click this button:

and you're offered AutoReport: Columnar and AutoReport: Tabular. Choose the former and then pick the ClubMembers table from the pop down list below.

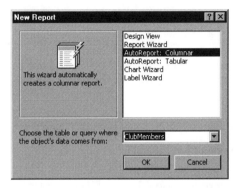

Click OK and the new report is displayed as shown below.

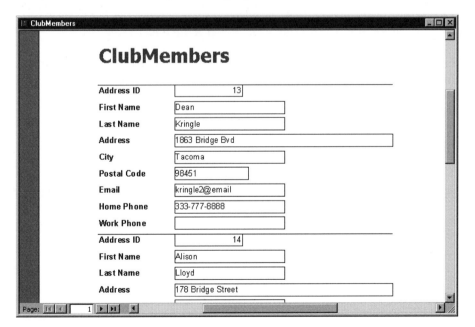

This columnar report has the same problems as the first AutoReport we generated. Throw it away and try the AutoReport: Tabular option which is sometimes more satisfactory, as it is here,

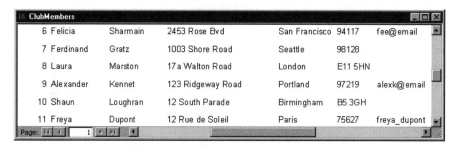

ClubMembers						
6 Felicia	Sharmain	2453 Rose Bvd	San Francisco	94117	fee@email	
7 Ferdinand	Gratz	1003 Shore Road	Seattle	98128		
8 Laura	Marston	17a Walton Road	London	E11 5HN		
9 Alexander	Kennet	123 Ridgeway Road	Portland	97219	alexk@email	
10 Shaun	Loughran	12 South Parade	Birmingham	B5 3GH		
11 Freya	Dupont	12 Rue de Soleil	Paris	75627	freya_dupont	

Page: ◄◄ ◄ 1 ► ►► ◄

but I still won't save it as once more the records are in entry order rather than alphabetical by surname: the `PhoneList` report does a much better job.

Printing a report

OK, you've created a report, now let's get it committed to paper. We're presuming you have a printer set up from Windows and ready to go.

❥ *Troubleshooting printer problems is outside the remit of this book but if you experience difficulties, start by checking your printer setup under Windows.* ❧

First let's have a sneak preview of what we hope will roll out of the printer. In the Reports tab, highlight the `PhoneList` report and click either the Preview button in the database window or the Print Preview button on the toolbar. (Hint: use hover help and look left).

Your report is displayed just as it will look on paper. (Click the One Page button to see the whole page).

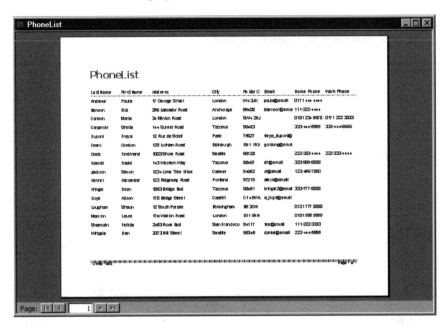

It looks promising so click the Print button on the toolbar. Your report should print out looking just like the preview with a title at the top and the data arranged under field headings, with today's date and a page number at the bottom.

Summary

You can now print out reports from your database – membership lists, monthly sales reports and personal phone directories are just a few clicks away.

Chapter 7

The story so far

You can create and manage a simple database

With the tools and techniques covered in the preceding chapters you can create and manage a simple database for such applications as club membership, inventories and address/contact lists. You can do everything from building the database to the point when you can present neat printed reports of the information collected.

You've met the four important building blocks

Tables – for storing data

Queries – for locating specific information

Forms – for interacting with the data (viewing, adding or editing records)

Reports – for presenting printed information

These four will appear again as we continue our progress through Access and each time they surface you'll learn a little more about them. While it's true that things get more complex from here on in, Access' famed ease of use rarely falters.

Revisit the big four

In the next five chapters we'll take a longer, harder look at each of the components in turn, explaining capabilities and demonstrating their use. This will let you hone your simple database to the peak of perfection where only fine upstanding data is permitted to enter its hallowed table, where stylish forms beckon the user, where queries surprise and reports satisfy. Enough of this hyperbole; here comes Chapter 8.

Part III

Creating hand-crafted databases

Chapter 8

Exploring tables in more depth

What more could you possibly need to know?

So far we've looked at the quick and easy routes to creating tables provided by Access wizards. They offer a degree of flexibility which will cover the needs of most simple databases and if you never feel the need to delve any further, that's fine. However, databases frequently develop over time. Once the basics are in place and a table is used in earnest, all sorts of other possibilities and ideas pop up and these go beyond what's possible at the level described thus far.

When a wizard isn't enough

There are things that the wizards can't do but Access is full of extra functionality to do practically everything you can imagine. For instance, it's perfectly possible to ensure that only 'Mr' and 'Ms' are permitted as entries in a `Title` field (though whatever titles you choose these days, someone somewhere will be offended). It's not difficult to set this up but you can't do it with a wizard.

Modifying a wizard's work

Even when your needs outstrip those met by wizards, they are still very useful. You can use the Table wizard to build the basic data storage table and then you can add further refinements to that table using the other tools Access provides (as we did with the `TestCalc` form in Chapter 5). However, in order to make meaningful changes to the structure of a table you need some background information.

Primary keys

You have already found that Access is almost obsessed with primary keys; every time you use the Table wizard Access tries to make sure that you add one. A primary key is a field (or fields) that contains a unique value for each record. For example, you might have a table of employees within a company. Each person will have a national insurance number (UK), social security number (US) or equivalent, that is unique to that person. So if you decide to include a field in the table which holds that number, then that field is perfect as a primary key. Unlike people, most items aren't issued with a government-defined number (thankfully). However, items used within a company are often numbered for convenience by that company – think about order numbers, part numbers etc. Again, these are often chosen to be the primary key value in a table. Even if you create a table of information about your friends and relations, it's a good idea to give the table a primary key. This doesn't mean that you have to find out your cousin's social security number, you can simply set up a field called, perhaps, ID and put a 1 in that field for the first record, a 2 for the second and so on.

This tells us what a primary key does – the value in the primary key field uniquely identifies every record in the table. But it doesn't tell us **why** each table needs a primary key. The answer is that primary keys are essential when we start to use multiple tables together in a single database. We'll start to do that in Part IV whereupon primary keys will begin to make more sense. However, we will still be making sure as we work that every table has a primary key. The field chosen by the Table wizard during the building of a table, or when you save a manually-built table, will be fine.

Incidentally, I said above that 'a primary key is a field (or fields)' and this is perfectly true – a primary key can be made up of two or more fields, although it is often composed of just one. We'll touch on this again in Chapter 15 in the section called Many-To-Many relationships.

Data types

Tables store data and data comes in many different flavors. Access lets you determine the type of data that will be stored in each field and it is a good idea to try to match the data type to the type of data (if you see what I mean!) that you intend to store in that field. As a simple example, suppose that you create a table of the stock held in a warehouse. The table might be called 'stock' and have three fields – `PartNumber`, `Name` and `Stock`:

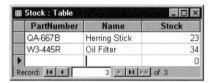

If we ignore `PartNumber` for the moment, it is clear that `Name` is supposed to contain text-type information and `Stock` (the number of items in stock) is destined to contain numbers. Therefore, the data type for `Name` is text and the data type for `Stock` is number. Simple. In fact, telling Access what data types to use brings several benefits.

For a start, Access can prevent you from putting the wrong data into a field:

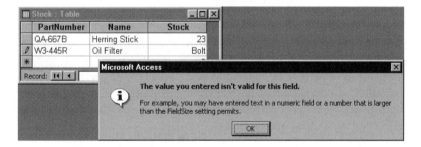

In addition, choosing the right data type can save storage space, making your database leaner and faster as we'll explain at the end of the chapter.

So data types are worth knowing about and we'll look at each of the data types and the sort of data you'd store in each. The table below lists all the possible types.

Data type	Field size property
Text	
Number	Byte
	Integer
	Long Integer
	Single
	Double
	Replication ID
	Decimal
Date/Time	
Currency	
AutoNumber	Long Integer
Yes/No	
Lookup wizard	
Hyperlink	
OLE Object	
Memo	

The number data type is subdivided into seven field sizes for dealing with different numerical ranges (see below). Some are very much more commonly used than others. It's useful to have a feel for everything that Access **can** handle but you'll probably find that you mainly use long integer and single in practice, so you probably don't need to spend too long studying the different types that are on offer.

To demonstrate data types, we'll create a table called DataTypes in a new database of the same name. From the Tables tab in the database window, double click 'Create table in design view'.

You're now in an entirely blank table design area where you can define the fields.

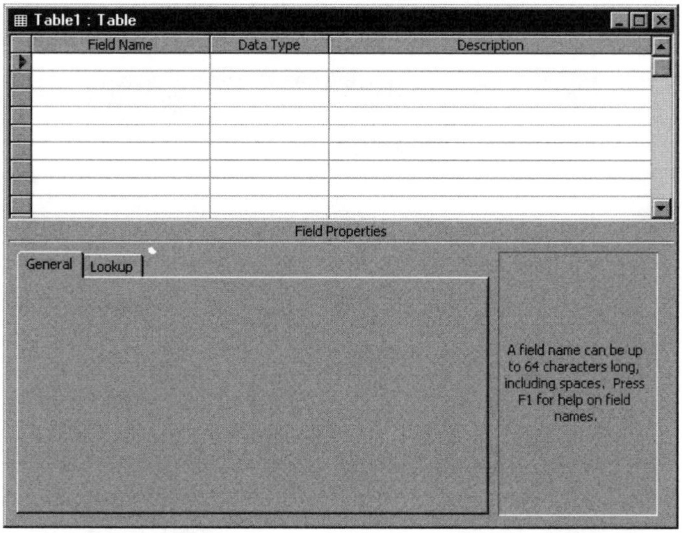

The top panel of the dialog is divided into rows and columns. Field names, data types and descriptions are entered here. Beneath this lies the Field Property panel where the properties of each field are defined. The box to the right displays handy tips, determined by the position of the cursor.

Selecting data types

In the Field Name column, type a name for the field: we'll use Text.

❛ *Clearly using the name of the data type isn't normally to be recommended, you'd use a name like* `FirstName` *or* `CompanyName`*, but we've designed this table just to demonstrate the different data types.* ❜

Press the right arrow key, or Enter, or click in the adjacent cell in the Data Type column. The default data type is Text, which happens to be fine. However, just to show you how it works, click the arrow button at the right of the cell,

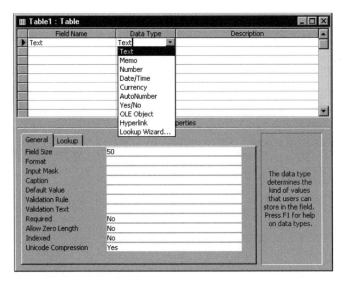

and a list of all available data types pops down. If you wanted something other than text for this field, you'd select it here.

Add a few words about the field in the Description column if you wish; this isn't obligatory but can be helpful if field names are vague. Hint: don't use vague field names!

Data type: Text

A field of the text data type is used for storing text: no surprises there. Names, addresses, descriptions of products, colors and countries would sit happily in the text category. Numbers as well as characters can be entered in text fields as in an address like 1054 Penguin Boulevard. The numbers in an address are like a label; they're never used mathematically. (When did you last calculate the average house number of your friends?) Indeed, the different ways in which numbers are used generally is worth bearing in mind. Phone numbers are numerical, but as you never multiply one by another, they are more properly stored in a text field. This prevents other problems too. Any leading zeros (which every number has if the full international rendition is used) are truncated by numerical formats. Also, it's common to use spaces, dashes and even brackets in phone numbers and these are disallowed in any of the numerical field types. So, always store telephone numbers in a text field unless you have a very good reason to do otherwise.

Serial numbers and other codes used for identification are always stored as text if they contain any text characters. Only if they are entirely numerical (without any leading zeros!) is it reasonable to store them in a field of type Number.

The table below shows examples of text data.

Field name	Data type	Example entry
Surname	Text	Campbell
Address	Text	124 East Street
State	Text	CA
Serial Number	Text	TFH1567-8/R
Phone Number	Text	(375) 344-444
Fax Number	Text	001 535 890 745
License Number	Text	XGN 845 G
Stock Code	Text	0000345

So, in the `Stock` table mentioned above, it should now be clear that the `PartNumber` field, despite having 'Number' in the field name, should actually be of data type text.

❡ *The text data type can also be called an alphanumeric data type. This is perhaps a better term as it makes it clear that as well as holding letters of the alphabet, numbers can be stored too.* ❡

Data type: Memo

This is a useful data type for fields with a large but variable amount of alphanumeric text, such as additional notes or background information. Up to 64,000 characters can be stored, but happily the space taken up is determined by the length of the entry so none is wasted by storing shorter entries or by not having an entry for some, or even most, records. If you were creating a table of data about restaurants, you would store the establishment's name in a text field but notes about the ambiance in a memo field. The entries in memo fields can be searched but cannot be indexed (see below). Add a memo field called Memo to the table.

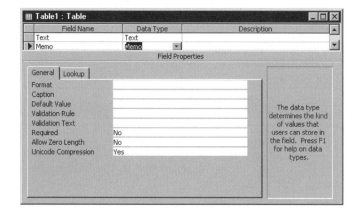

Data type: Number

When you select the data type Number, the Field Property panel allows you to select one of seven separate Field Sizes which are outlined briefly in the table below.

Field size	Range	Decimal places	Storage space/record
Byte	0–255	0	1 byte
Integer	–32,768 to 32,767	0	2 bytes
Long Integer	–2,147,483,648 to 2,147,483,647	0	4 bytes
Single	-3.4×10^{38} to 3.4×10^{38}	7	4 bytes
Double	-1.797×10^{308} to 1.797×10^{308}	15	8 bytes
Decimal	$-10^{28} - 1$ to $10^{28} - 1$	28	12 bytes
Replication ID	globally unique identifiers (see below)	NA	16 bytes

❢ *When is a data type not a data type? Sticking strictly to Access's terminology, Number is a data type and its subdivisions (byte, integer et al.) are field sizes. In common parlance, however, byte, integer and so on are referred to as data types so we'll stick with that.* ❢

These seven data types have different properties, notably different storage requirements. At the end of this chapter is a discussion of storage requirements vs. speed.

Selecting the field size

Type in the field name 'Number'. The data type defaults to text so click the button in the Data Type column and select Number. In the Field Properties panel, the General tab is current and the first item in its list is Field Size. The default is Long Integer. Click to place the cursor in the field size cell and click on the button that appears. A list of seven choices pops down. Make your selection here.

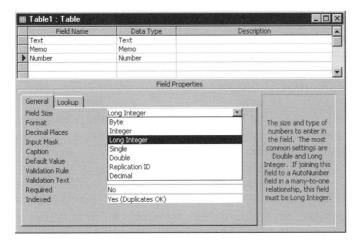

❢ *We are about to enumerate all of the numerical data types for the sake of completeness. If you aren't mathematically inclined this may begin to get tedious. If it does, use the following simple rule: most whole numbers can be stored happily in the default type which is Long Integer. If your number is going to include decimal values (like 1.23) then choose Single. If that sounds fine for the moment, feel free to skip to the section headed **Data type: Date/Time**.* ❢

Data type: Number – Byte

Many pieces of data fall within the bounds of the byte field: it's perfect for household inventory fields, for instance. Even the cleanest family is unlikely to hit the 255 limit for washing machines and such devices rarely occur in thirds or halves. Byte cannot store negative numbers... but that is OK for washing machines as well.

Data type: Number – Integer

Useful for numbers that can be negative and that also have a range greater than 255 but less than 32,000 odd. Great for the number of pupils in a school or employees in a small to medium sized enterprise.

Data type: Number – Long Integer

Long Integer is the default data type. Even larger numbers can be stored in the long integer data type (minus two to plus two million and then some) and many applications will never approach the upper or lower limit. Useful for order numbers for a reasonable sized company. You still can't store decimal places in this field type so a number like 3.14159 is right out.

Data type: Number – Single

These numbers are getting ever more vast but, perhaps more importantly, you can finally store decimal values so you can enter a number like 3.14159. Up to seven decimal places are permitted.

Data type: Number – Double

Even more mind-stretchingly huge numbers can be stored in the double field type. Given that there are about 10^{73} particles in the observable universe (last time I looked) the limit of 1.797×10^{308} is probably adequate for most purposes. This data type can also store even more decimal places. Wow.

Data type: Number – Decimal

This one's for huge numbers where high levels of precision are required. Numbers can be quoted to 28 decimal places which should be enough for most mortals.

Data type: Number – Replication ID

The replication ID field stores globally unique identifiers (GUIDs for short and possibly pronounced like 'good' with a strong Scottish accent? Whatever.) GUIDs are used to identify the components of a database for use in the process of replication.

❧ *In a nutshell, replication helps to allow users who are disconnected from a shared database to work with data from that database. The bottom line is that if you are new to Access you probably don't want to worry about this data type yet.* ❧

So there are lots of different numerical data types. Choose whichever one takes your fancy for the table you are creating.

Data type: Date/Time

If you want to store a date, you might argue that you simply need to use a text field because in there you can type 'January 1 2001'. True, you can. The problem with doing this is that Access will store it for you as text and won't be able to perform so-called 'Date Arithmetic' on that date. For example, it won't be able to work out that there are 36 days between the 1st of January and the 7th of February in the same year, or that if Helen's date of birth is the 12th of September 1963, on the 22nd of October 1999 she was 36. We manipulate dates all the time and we often want Access to do the same for us. However, in order for Access to do this, we have to use a Date/Time field.

❧ *When a date is entered into a Date/time field, it is actually stored behind the scenes as a number and Access uses that number to work out the answers we want. For example, the date 17th June 1999 is stored as 36328. The same is true for time: you can't just type 15:24 in a text field and hope that Access knows it is temporal information meaning 'getting on for half past three and time for a cup of tea'. Instead you type, say, '17 June 1999 15:24' into a time/date field and Access will store it as 36328.6416666667* ❧

Date and time data can be displayed in different ways; these are covered in the following pages. Add a field called Date/Time to the table. In fact, add one of the appropriate name for the rest of the data types once you've read the descriptions below.

Data type: Currency

This is just what it seems, a field for storing values which equate to currency values. Up to four decimal places are permitted, with up to 15 digits before the decimal point.

Data type: AutoNumber

This data type generates a series of numbers automatically, incremented by one. The most common use for this is as an ID field for use as a primary key. So, after you have added an AutoNumber field called AutoNumber to your table, with the cursor still on that field, click on the Primary Key button (the one with the key symbol). The field should acquire a key symbol at the left hand side of the table.

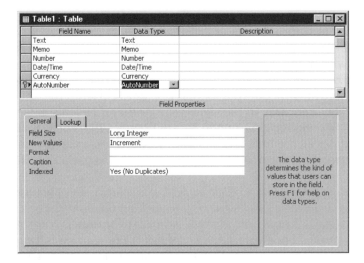

It is conventional (but not essential) to put the primary key field(s) at the top of the table. You can move fields around as follows. Click on the key symbol to the left of the AutoNumber field and the entire row should highlight.

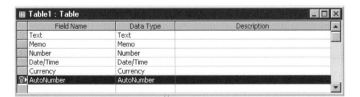

Release the mouse button, and then click in the same place, but hold the mouse button down. Now slide the row upwards to the top of the table and then release the mouse button.

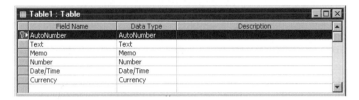

As I said, you don't have to follow this convention but it does make life easier (you always know where to find the primary key) so why flout accepted wisdom?

When you tell the Table wizard that you want it to provide a primary key, it adds an `ID` field of the AutoNumber data type to the table. Every time you add a record, Access assigns it the next number in sequence and writes it into the `AutoNumber` field.

The AutoNumber data type is, in fact, simply a specialized form of Long Integer field so the values stored in an AutoNumber field are actually just long integers. You may feel that you don't really need to know this, but this factoid becomes important when we start using multiple tables.

Data type: Yes/No

There are many pieces of information that are either one thing or the other, without shades in between (for database purposes, anyway – human beings are past masters of 'yes, but...' exceptions.) Do you have a current driving license? Have you ever been in Canada? The Yes/No data type stores the response neatly in a mere 1 bit. (In other words, the information is stored very efficiently, which means that less disk space is wasted.) Once again, like dates, you could use a text field and store 'Yes' or 'No' but it is better to use a Yes/No data type because then people won't enter 'Yup', 'Yo' or any other unhelpful variant. A Yes/No field will, by default, accept simply a tick for yes and a lack of a tick for no so people can input the information using a mouse.

Data type: OLE Object

OLE stands for Object Linking and Embedding – this data type allows you to link to, or embed, an object from outside Access into a table. Such an object might be an Excel spreadsheet, a Word document or an image. So if you had a spreadsheet holding details of employees' expenses, you could access it from within Access using a field of the OLE Object data type.

Data type: Hyperlink

This data type is potentially useful for the web aware. A hyperlink field can contain a URL so your table could contain the location of a person's home page. Any entries in this field are formatted to appear blue and underlined, the classic look for URLs. Hyperlink fields can also contain UNC paths to point to a specific file either on your PC or on a server.

❢ *A URL is a Uniform Resource Locator and is used to point to a specific place.* `http://www.msn.com` *is a typical URL. A UNC path is Universal Naming Convention path which acts in a similar way but points to a shared folder and file on a PC or file server, like this:* `\\machine\folder\filename.mdb`. ❢

Hyperlink fields are obviously seen as an important option in Access as there are short cut methods of inserting these fields into the Datasheet view of a table and hyperlinks themselves into the hyperlink field. To perform the first of these short cuts you simply click on Insert, Hyperlink Column and bingo, there it is with a default field name that can be edited to suit.

To place a hyperlink in a hyperlink column in the table, click Insert and then Hyperlink (or Control-K from the keyboard). This window opens, letting you browse to the required file or page.

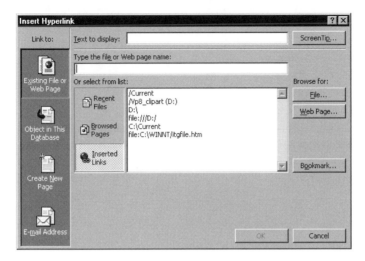

Clicking OK puts the UNC path or URL into the table.

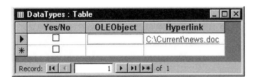

Data type: Lookup wizard

The Lookup wizard isn't really a data type but it appears in the data type combo box so we've included it here. This is a very useful device for keeping data within bounds. The Lookup wizard gives you complete control over the entries that are allowed in that field. If you only want the responses Blue, Green, Red or Purple in a field, use the Lookup wizard type. You can either determine the permitted entries when you're building the field with the wizard or you can set the field to refer automatically to data from another table.

91

Type in a field name and select the Lookup wizard. The wizard runs and asks where the permissible values will come from.

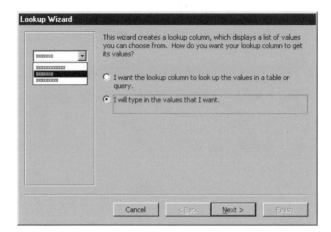

We'll try typing in the values so choose this and click Next. The wizard suggests a default of one column. In the single column table start typing the allowable entries; as soon as you start typing an entry, a new row appears in the table. Build up a 'table' looking like this.

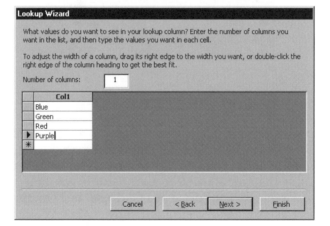

Click Next, type a name for the lookup column (for this example it's
`ColorList`) and click Finish. The data type has reverted to text (but see
below). Check out the properties in the Lookup tab and in the Row Source
cell you'll see the valid entries. Notice also that the Field Name has
changed to reflect the name you gave the lookup column.

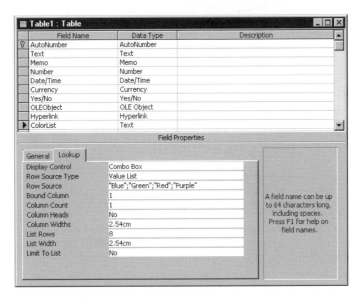

Click to save the table and swop to the Datasheet view. When the cursor is
place in the `ColorList` field, a button appears giving access to the list of
permitted entries.

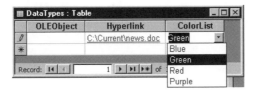

If you try to type in anything other than these precise entries, you'll find you can, which seems to negate the whole idea. Swop to Design view and check out the last property on the Lookup tab. It says 'Limit to list'. Aah. Click to see the options and select Yes.

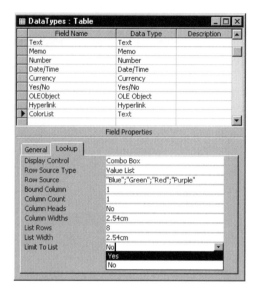

Back in table view, try entering Mauve. Access beeps when you try to leave the field and the message window tells you to pick one from the list.

Your lookup list is now functioning and will not permit entries other than those you specified.

In our example, we accepted the default data type which was text but you don't have to do this. You might, for example, provide the values 1, 2 and 3 and then set the data type to numeric: it's up to you. However, if you do something logically questionable, like setting up a list of colors and then set the data type to be numeric, Access will, quite reasonably, object when you try to enter data.

❛ *You can also run the Lookup wizard in the Design view by clicking on Insert in the main menu and choosing Lookup Field...* ❜

Summary so far

We have had a look at the different data types that are available in Access, and a sample table, DataTypes, containing examples of each is available in the file called chap8datatypes.mdb. You can create a form for this table using AutoForm and then play around entering data into the different fields. Most of the results that you get will be self-explanatory as soon as you see the end result. However, a couple of points may be worth noting. One is that you can enter text into the hyperlink field and if you double click on the entry, Windows will try to connect you to that URL. If you use an ISP (Internet Service Provider) then your machine is likely to try and establish a contact with that provider.

Another point is that if you want to insert an object into the OLE field, click on the field and the select Insert, Object and then use the dialog box to choose the options you want.

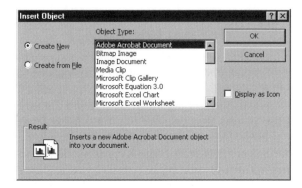

It is worth spending some time playing with this until you are happy that you have a feel for the sort of data that is best suited to the different data types that Access offers.

Controlling data entry

OK, so you now know how to construct a table that can hold the correct **type** of data. The next stage is to learn how you can modify the table so that, as far as is feasible, only **correct** data ends up in that table. To be of real value, your data must be as accurate as possible. Unfortunately, most data is entered by people and people don't always function with 100% accuracy. Access recognizes that we're only human and provides several ways of improving the accuracy of data that gets into a database.

One way, which we have already covered, is to use the lookup wizard. Users no longer stare at a field labeled 'Grade' wondering whether they should enter 'A++', 'Yes' or 'NA'; they're able to pick an answer from the range supplied.

❦ *Controlled data entry also helps keep humorists in check. No longer will a field labeled 'Sex?' hold such side-splitting entries as 'Yes please'. Not that I have anything against humor, indeed if I had to lose one or the other then databases would have to go. With any luck though, we should be able to keep both.* ❦

Another way in which Access can help is to look for an expected pattern in the incoming data, which bring us to input masks, as mentioned briefly in Chapter 3.

Input masks – the background

An input mask lets you control data entry into a field to a remarkable degree. Using such a mask you can ensure that, for example, phone numbers are always entered in the format (123) 456-789 or that data always conforms to a required pattern, such as two characters followed by a dash and then three numbers. This is particularly useful for numbers that are forced upon us by bureaucracy: social security numbers, license numbers, permit numbers and so on. They are also invaluable within companies where you may know that, for instance, part numbers always conform to the format AA-111.

The mask itself

The input mask is built up from various characters and symbols which acquire a special meaning in the context of masks. These are shown below.

Character/symbol	Description of action
0	digit (0–9, entry compulsory)
9	digit or space (entry optional)
#	digit or space (optional; blank positions appear as spaces)
L	letter (A–Z, compulsory)
?	letter (A–Z, optional)
A	letter or digit ()
a	letter or digit (optional)
&	any character or a space (compulsory)
C	any character or a space (optional)
. , : ; - /	Decimal point, thousands, date and time separators
<	all subsequent characters will appear in lowercase
>	all subsequent characters will appear in uppercase
!	causes the input mask to display from right to left, reversing the default. Can be positioned anywhere in the mask
\	the subsequent character is displayed literally. Displays any of the characters listed in this table as literal characters (i.e. \& appears as &)

If you wanted a serial number field to contain entries in the format three uppercase characters, dash, five numbers (ABC-12345), the mask would look like this:

>LLL\-00000

If serial numbers like AB-123 and A-1 were also valid (i.e. with variable numbers of letters and digits, though at least one of each) the mask would look like this:

>L??\-09999

Creating an input mask

Create a new table, add a text field called PhoneNumber and, in the General Field Properties, you should find a property called Input Mask. Type in the following:

\(000") "000\-0000

There is no immediate reason why this cannot be a primary key field, so, in your best *Star Trek* manner, make it so.

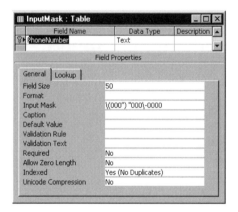

❦ *You can in fact, type*

(000) 000-0000

and Access will presume the brackets, space and dash to be literal and show the mask as

\(000") "000\-0000   ❥

You should then find that you can only enter numbers in the form:

(123) 123-1234

Input masks are easy to create and efficient in use. If required, you can invoke a wizard to create some for you, just by pressing the ellipsis button (the one with three dots) that appears in the last but one screen shot. However, it is essentially just as easy to create your own.

In fact, input masks can be made more complex that this. They can have three separate elements with the other two bits allowing a degree of fine control that's not used all that commonly. They're covered in a section called 'More on input masks' towards the end of the chapter but it certainly isn't required reading at this stage.

Investigating the main properties of fields

Objects have properties and the fields in an Access table are no exception. The properties of each field in a table can be set from the Design view, more specifically in the Field Properties panel.

The list of properties varies with the data type of the field; number fields have a Field Size property, as already discussed. Other data types lack this property but are imbued with others. We'll have a look at the main properties – these are the ones that you're most likely to need to understand when getting to grips with table design.

Format

Every data type except OLE Object has a format property with predefined formats for the date/time data type.

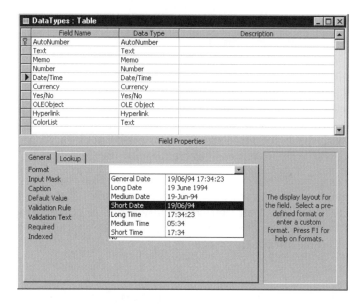

❝ *The Short Date format assumes dates between 1/1/00 and 12/31/29 are in the years 2000 to 2029. Dates between 1/1/30 and 12/31/99 are assumed to be twentieth century dates, i.e. the years 1930 to 1999.* ❞

To demonstrate the various date/time formats we have created a table where they are set differently, called `DateTimeFormats`, and below is a form with the same name to display them.

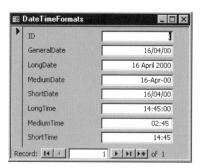

❝ *We happen to be doing this in the UK where the Windows default is set to dd/mm/yyyy rather than mm/dd/yyyy. So 12/01/1967 is the 12th January 1967 rather than 1st December 1967.* ❞

Predefined formats are also available for the currency data type.

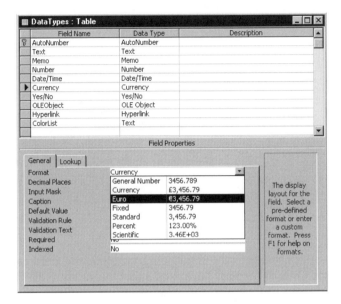

All currency fields also have a Decimal Places property which can be set to the desired accuracy.

The Yes/No data type also has three formats:

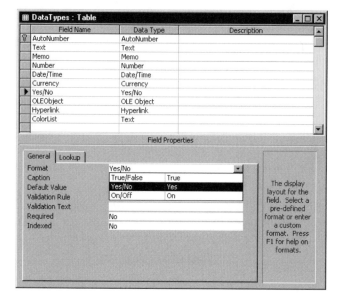

If it's more appropriate to the data being entered, the field can be set to True/False or On/Off format. True, Yes and On are equivalent responses and False, No and Off are also equivalents.

❻ *When storing Yes/No data, Access uses –1 to mean Yes and 0 to equal No. This sounds positively perverse to the non-mathematical though, in fact, there is a deeply theoretical and (reasonably) reasonable for this choice. For an easy life let's just accept the weirdness hit.* ❾

So, what is the point we are trying to make about formatting? There is an important distinction between the data type and the format. The data type controls the data that can be entered into a field, the format property controls the way in which the data appears to the user. In a sense the former provides an absolute control over the value stored, the latter simply controls how the value is perceived. The two can be used in a variety of ways. For example, you may well want to store some values to a high degree of accuracy, but display them with only integer accuracy. This can be achieved by mixing and matching the data type and the format.

Caption

All field types have a caption property. If you enter a caption, it will be used as the field label in any form based upon the table. If you don't use captions your fields are still labeled because the field name will be used instead.

Captions can be up to 2,048 characters long, which is more than enough for most uses.

Default Value

This property is held by all fields except AutoNumber and OLE Object.

The Default Value property specifies a text string or a number that will appear automatically in a field when a new record is created. For example, if most of your customers are based in Switzerland you might have a `Country` text field with the default value set to 'Switzerland'.

When you need an entry for another country, you simply start typing. The default entry is highlighted when your cursor arrives in the field and is deleted as soon as you type.

The maximum length for a default value is 255 characters. A default value can also be an expression; these are covered below.

Validation Rule

Like Default Value, this property is ascribed to all fields except AutoNumber and OLE Object. Access undertakes some data validation automatically, precluding text from being entered into any of the number fields, for instance. If you want a further level of validation, you can set a rule by which any entry must abide.

For example, imagine you run a Botanic Garden, need to store the date on which a plant variety was acquired and want to ensure that it always falls between the date you started your collection and today's date. We can demonstrate this using the Date/Time field in the `DataTypes` table.

Open the table in Design mode, click in the Validation Rule row and enter the expression:

Between #01/01/89# And Date()

❻ *Hints: 'Between' is a comparison operator. 'Date' is a built-in date/time function that supplies the current date.*

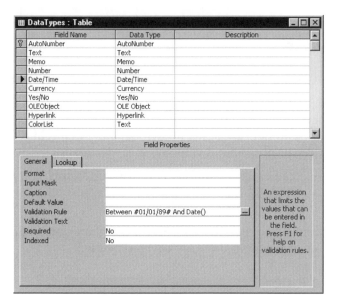

If you've just added a couple of records for experimentation purposes as we go along you may see the following message when you save the table:

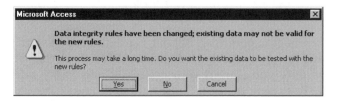

Click Yes and it should take a mere moment for Access to test them with the new validation rule.

If you try to enter a date that is outside these limits, Access refuses to accept it.

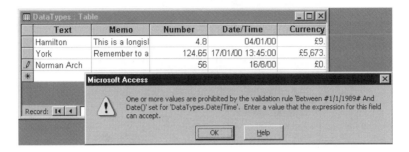

Incidentally, Access provides an Expression Builder to help you to compose expressions like this. You can get it by clicking on the Build button – that's the one with the ellipsis that appears when your cursor is in place to enter a Validation Rule.

Click the Build button and the Expression Builder appears. Here you can hunt through the functions

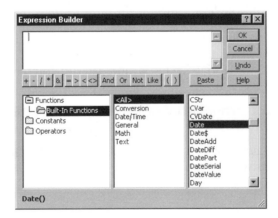

and operators

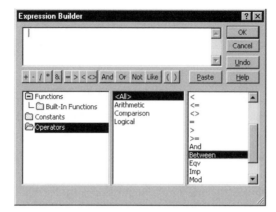

and build the expression you want by pasting in your choices instead of typing everything in. This builder can be particularly useful when you are starting to use Access and aren't familiar with all the functions and operators that are available.

Validation Text

The Validation Text property goes hand in hand with the Validation Rule property. You can define the message seen by users if an attempt is made to enter data which does not conform to the validation rule. 'Try again, dummy' probably won't win any prizes for diplomacy; 'Ensure the date is between 01/01/89 and today's date' is more tactful. You have 255 characters in which to express yourself.

If you set a validation rule but no validation text, Access displays a standard error message when the rule is violated (see above).

Type the error message you want into the validation text slot. The error message appears with a warning triangle if invalid data is entered.

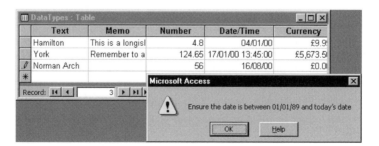

Required

The property Required can be set to either Yes or No. If an entry into a field is obligatory, set this property to Yes. If you must know whether a person was born in Italy to make any sense of the rest of the data collected, ensure the Required property is set to Yes.

Indexing

This property lets you define what is called an 'Index' on a field. Indexes (more correctly indices but most people say indexes) are wonderful. Suppose you have a table that stores a list of the employees in your company. You regularly search through this looking for particular people, locating them using their last name. If you put an index on the `LastName` field, your searches will run much faster, often by one or more orders of magnitude!

The three options are shown below; the default is No index.

Setting	Description
No index	
Yes (Duplicates OK)	The index permits duplicates
Yes (No Duplicates)	The index doesn't permit duplicates

For use with the `LastName` field the 'Yes (Duplicates OK)' would be the one to choose as it's quite possible you'd have employees with identical last names.

Primary keys are, by default, indexed automatically in Access with the 'Yes (No Duplicates)' option. Access also lets you have as many other indexes as you want so you may be tempted to index every field immediately. However, each index you create takes up some disk space and, with a large table, too many indexes can slow down data entry. So use them sparingly but on the other hand don't be afraid to use them because the speed gains are tremendous.

❛ *You will notice that we are saying, in effect, that there is no hard and fast rule here. You will have to use your judgement and/or you will have to experiment to find the best balance of indexes for a particular database. As you start to build more complex databases, these judgement calls (about indexes and other components) become more important. This is why, for me at least, designing databases is such a delight; it becomes both a science and an art. There is real satisfaction in creating a fast, elegant database.* ❜

107

Having said that, there is one place where an index is almost always worth applying and that is a foreign key field. You haven't met these yet, but they are covered in Chapter 15.

Summary of field properties

Field properties allow you to modify the way in which your table behaves. We haven't covered all of the possible options, but we have covered those properties that you're likely to need for the first databases you build. As you gain experience it's worth having a look at the rest of the properties to find out what they do.

Choosing the right data type means leaner, faster databases... up to a point

We said earlier that choosing the correct data type could make your database leaner and faster. To a large extent this has to do with size. If you want to store, say, the number of children that people have, you could choose the Byte data type (which would be the most appropriate). Choosing Decimal is a mistake because a user of your database might enter 3.187. Accepting Long Integer (the default) would be OK, except that it takes 4 bytes of storage space per record. I don't know anyone with two million children (nor with minus two million) and the 255 allowed by Byte are probably enough. So, Byte is fine, but what does it matter if you choose Long Integer? The answer is – it depends; it is a matter of judgment.

Look at it this way. Choosing Long Integer wastes 3 bytes per record. If you expect your table to have, say, 1,000,000 records, then your table will be 3,000,000 bytes = 3 Megabytes larger than if you had chosen Byte. Those extra 3 Mbytes matter, both in terms of storage and database speed. But if your table is only likely to have 50 records, then the wastage is trivial and not worth worrying about.

In the bad old days when computers struggled for disk space and power, we advocated choosing data types with great care. Given the power and capacity of modern PCs, we think it is foolish to worry unless your databases are likely to become huge. Be aware of the issue but don't become obsessed.

Summary

In this chapter, we've introduced data types and properties, two major methods of ensuring that the data in your tables is accurate. Using the most suitable data types for your data means that it can be handled quickly and accurately by Access. The properties of the fields in a table let you control entries as they're typed in and how they look once they're in.

Playing with the various data types and properties with a dummy database is an excellent way to get a feel for what they all do.

Not required on voyage

❢ *The information in the remainder of this chapter isn't required reading for your first database. However, it expands some of the topics covered in this chapter. For your first run through the book we actively advise that you don't read it but it may be useful for reference purposes later.* ❢

More on input masks

We said that input masks have three elements and that the first is the most useful and is covered above. As for the other two...

Displaying separation characters

The second element of the input mask determines whether the literal separation characters (like - and /) are stored in the field. These characters are often used to make the information more readable but it's not always necessary to store them.

There are two options for this:

- a 0 stores separation characters with the values
- a 1 (or a blank) stores values without separators

This element of the input mask is placed after a semi colon. So, for example, if we use this mask:

(000) 000-0000;0

numbers will be stored like this

(123) 456-789

in the table, but a mask like this:

(000) 000-0000;1

numbers will be stored like so

123456789.

❧ *Unfortunately, Access's super-helpful interface shows entries made with both these input masks as looking identical when data is viewed in the table. The brackets, space and dash appear for numbers input under both masks. Only when you, for example, export a table to Excel does the difference in the way the numbers are stored become apparent. In the screen shot below, the* PhoneNo *column contains data input with separation characters stored and the* PhoneNo2 *column contains data input stored without the separation characters.*

,

Displaying blanks

The third element determines the character that's displayed in the input mask to indicate where the entry should be typed: this character is known as a placeholder. You can use any character, for instance, *, displays a star character. If you omit the third element, the default character is the underscore (_).

These are examples of complete input masks:

(000) 000-0000;0
(000) AAA-AAAA;0;*
>L0L 0L0

And now more about the properties of a field...

Nulls

We are about to have a look at the Allow Zero Length property but before we do, we need to cover the topic of 'Nulls', primarily because a zero length string is mainly defined in terms of 'not being a null' and if you haven't met nulls yet, this definition will be totally unhelpful.

OK, so what is a null? Well, consider this statement as (allegedly) heard on a radio station. 'Well, it's good news for all you hay fever sufferers – the pollen count today is zero... because all the pollen counters are on strike.'

The joke has an added piquancy for database fanatics because it hinges on the confusion between a value and a null value. A well-designed database recognizes the fact that some data may be unavailable to the database and that uncollected data is **not** the same as zero. You would never really enter a zero if the pollen counters were on strike: so the field for today's pollen count would, instead, contain a null.

Imagine now that you are entering data into a table (either directly, or via a form, it doesn't matter). The table has four fields and none of them has a default value. You move to a new record, put the cursor into one of the fields and enter a value. Then you save the record and close the table. You haven't explicitly put anything into the other three fields, so they have nothing in them. More correctly, the three fields contain null values.

So, back to the question, what is a null? A null is an absence of data. It is not a blank, it is not a zero, it is an absence of data.

Does this distinction matter to anyone other than hay fever sufferers? Yes. Suppose that you have a class of thirty pupils. You have entered the name of each into an Access table which therefore has 30 records. You have marked 20 of their essays and placed those marks in the table, again in a field without a default value. So far so good. Now you ask Access for the average mark gained (this can be done with a query). Access adds up the marks so far and then divides that total by... what? 20 or 30? The answer is that Access knows that a null is not the same as a zero, it sees only 20 entries for the essay mark (despite the fact that there are 30 records) so it divides by 20. If you had set the default mark to be 0 then there would be thirty entries and Access would have divided by 30 and you would get the wrong answer.

Allow Zero Length

This property applies only to Text, Memo, and Hyperlink table fields and sounds simple but it is worth looking at in detail – which means we have to backtrack a little.

So first, what is a 'zero length string'? It's a field into which double quotation marks **without** a space between them have been entered. Oh, so it's a null. No, it is similar to, but not quite the same as, a null.

You could be forgiven for thinking that we are beginning to get very pedantic about all this, so consider a table that is used to collect names. We have four fields:

```
FirstName
SecondName
ThirdName
LastName
```

You start entering names. The first person has three forenames (even if the third one, St. John, looks strange)

Anthony Aloysius St. John Hancock

No problem, all four fields have entries.

The next person is John Smith. You don't know if he has a second and third name, so you enter the first and last. The result is that SecondName and ThirdName remain blank and therefore contain nulls. This is still fine.

Finally, Sally Jones appears. You happen to know her well and you know for a fact that she has no other names. So you leave the middle two fields blank. But wait, those fields now contain null values, exactly as they do for John Smith. But we **know** that Sally doesn't have middle names, which is not at all the same thing as being unsure. If you use a null it implies that you don't know. So, finally, we find out what a zero length string is for. You can use it for Sally's SecondName and ThirdName fields to mean 'We know about this value and it doesn't exist.'

The permutations of settings for Allow Zero Length and Required let you distinguish between null and zero length entries to prevent problems when fields are matched. A field that looks blank could also contain one or more space characters and these too, can be controlled, either allowing such entries in the field or not. The table below gives the permutations.

Required	Allow Zero Length	Action at data entry	Value stored
No	No	Enter pressed	Null
		Spacebar pressed	Null
		Zero length string entered	Not allowed
No	Yes	Enter pressed	Null
		Spacebar pressed	Null
		Zero length string entered	Zero length string
Yes	No	Enter pressed	Not allowed
		Spacebar pressed	Not allowed
		Zero length string entered	Not allowed
Yes	Yes	Enter pressed	Not allowed
		Spacebar pressed	Zero length string
		Zero length string entered	Zero length string

In order to let you play with these we have set up a table called `Nulls` which has four fields – one with each of these permutations – in the `chap8nulls.mdb` file.

Postal codes again (and phone numbers)

As described in Chapter 3, designing input masks for postal codes and phone numbers remains a nightmare.

Why? For a start, different countries use totally different systems (post codes in the UK, zip codes in the US to mention but two) and many databases need to store international information. Secondly, systems vary in complexity. The US coding system is much more logical than the Byzantine UK system of variable numbers of digits and letters in variable positions. You'll find, if you're using Access in the UK, that the mask on the ready-made postal code field offered by the Table wizard doesn't work, with valid codes like HR7 4PA being rejected. Users in the US will have a different mask on the postal codes field – and one that works.

Postal codes in the UK are much more complex that they initially appear. DD1 4HN is a valid postal code, so is W1A 4HG, but DD1A 4DD isn't. Sigh. In fact, it turns out to be impossible to construct an input mask that accepts all of the correct postcodes but rejects the invalid ones. If you are a really sad person, you may come to find this subject interesting. This happened to me (Mark) when I raised the subject in the database column that I write for the UK magazine *Personal Computer World* (*PCW*). Now it may be impossible to create an input mask that deals effectively with postcodes but, like most problems, it can be solved in other ways, such as using the programming language that's built in to Access. The subject rattled on for several months in the column with various people contributing ideas, information, suggestions and eventually snippets of code. I would include all of that information here, but I suspect that most people would find it boring. On the other hand, since the problem has been solved, it seems a shame not to include the information because some readers of the book are bound to need it. The solution is obvious. On the CD-ROM is a folder called `PostCodes`. In there is a text file containing some of the more interesting correspondence from readers of the column, together with some code samples. In addition, there are the original `.mdb` files that I built to demonstrate the solutions that people contributed. All of the code and samples are in Access 2.0 format but it seems to translate successfully to Access 2000. I haven't, however, rigorously checked this and it is all, of course, provided without any guarantees whatsoever. It seems to work but it is provided solely for demonstration purposes.

Phone numbers cause similar problems and again, in the UK version of Access, the masks for ready-made phone/fax number fields created by the Table wizard don't work. Once again there is some information relating to this in the `PostCodes` folder.

If you want to know more, read the document called `PostCodes.doc` and this will point you to, and tell you a bit about, the `.mdb` files.

Chapter 9

Tapping the power of Access queries

Queries are much more powerful than they first appear

Queries can show you exactly the aspect of your data that interests you, without a clutter of data that's irrelevant to the task in hand. Queries are also great for times when you're sure that certain information can be teased out of the database; it's so quick to build and modify queries that you can do it iteratively, narrowing your criteria until you reach the goal. It's also often possible to start from a wizard-generated query and speed up the process further.

So far we've talked about basing forms and reports on an underlying table of data, but one of Access' most powerful assets is its ability to base forms and reports on the answer table generated by a query. There's more on this topic later in the chapter.

Records extracted with a query can be sorted into a specified order, and as people prefer to deal with sorted information, this makes the assimilation of results easier. Listing customers by surname, for example, lets you check individual records quickly. Queries can also perform mathematical calculations and return the results. The values in a field can be summed, the number of values counted, averages calculated and so on. Bearing in mind that, as we've just said, forms can be based on queries, a world of possibilities opens up. You might, for instance, build a query that extracted all of the orders from Boston that your company has processed, calculated the total value of each order and then sorted them by that value. You could then base a form on that query called, say, `BigBostonOrders`. The people who use your database don't have to know how you have done this, all they need to know is that when they open the form they see the relevant data, neatly summed and sorted.

Sometimes a query will uncover some hitherto unknown aspect of your data; maybe you sell more red cars in the south of your territory and mainly blue ones in the north. Not only do queries let you extract more information from your raw data, they let you make more of the information you extract.

Once a database has been established and is in use, it will need to be maintained and this is another area where queries are invaluable. The so-called 'action' queries (see below) are used to automate housekeeping tasks which would be seriously tedious to perform manually.

So, if it sounds as if we are fans of queries, indeed, we are. A database doesn't begin to repay the effort required to create and maintain it until you start to extract information from it and queries are the main tools for that extraction.

The main types of query

So far, when looking at queries we've concentrated on Select queries which can extract subsets of the fields and the records. However, Select queries are not the only type we can run. In fact, there are five categories of query, ranging from the straightforward to the advanced. All are designed to let you find exactly what you want in your database and some have their own wizards. Very briefly (just to give you an overview) they are:

Type of query	Usage
Select	Selects fields/records from a table according to the criteria specified
Parameter	Displays dialog boxes which prompt the user to supply a criteria on which to query (parameter value criteria)
Range	Selects fields/records which contain a range of values
Group By and Crosstab	Displays summarized values (sums, counts, averages) in a grid form, looking much like a spreadsheet, taking its rows and columns from chosen fields.
Action	Performs actions to change the records in a table (Delete, Update and Append queries) and to create new tables (the Make-Table query)

And now we'll look at each in more detail.

Creating a Select query

You've already created select queries – we built these in Chapter 4 with the wizard and from the Design view.

Select queries are the simplest and most common type of query; they're also highly useful, letting you concentrate on a reduced set of the information in a database.

To re-cap briefly, the main steps are:

- Choose the table you wish to query.
- Choose the fields you want to use in the query.
- Add criteria to choose the records you wish to find.
- Run the query.

Creating a Parameter query

A parameter query is also amazingly useful, particularly when you know that you are going to have to query the same table many times but that you are going to be looking for slightly different sets of information each time. Suppose you have a table of customer records. You find that you frequently want to run a query that shows all of the records of the customers from a given city but that the city changes each time you run the query. One time you need to see all of the customers from Paris, then you need to see everyone in London, next time Boston and so on. Using a parameter query gives you a quick way of checking out records of different cities without having to edit the query in the Design window every time. When a parameter query runs a dialog box appears, you type in the appropriate city and the query is automatically set to search for records that match. This is invaluable when you are building a database for other people to use, particularly when they don't know how to build queries.

Parameter queries can prompt for more than one piece of information; if you commonly retrieve sales made within a period of time, you can design prompts to ask for the start and finish dates. With these entered, all records that lie between the two dates are retrieved by the query.

❻ *Incidentally, we said in Chapter 2 that reports and forms can be based on queries and that includes parameter queries. Reports that are required regularly (perhaps a monthly sales report) are well suited to being based on parameter queries. When such a report is run, it asks, by means of a dialog box, for the period the report is to cover. Enter the month and the report will automatically take the values from records from that period.* ❾

Returning to the Club database, we'll build a parameter query to select records for a city that you will specify in a dialog box once the query is running. Open the chap9start.mdb file and build a select query with the wizard.

Include the FirstName, LastName and City fields from the ClubMembers table in the query and call it CityPeople. When the wizard displays the answer table, swop to Design view. Prepare to add a criteria to the City field but instead of the usual 'London', type the text that you want the parameter query dialog to display. This text must be wrapped in square brackets. '[Type in the city:]' is the text used here.

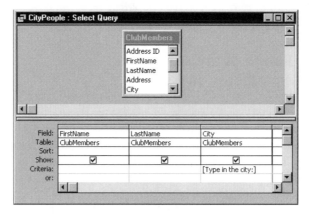

Run the query to see the completed dialog box.

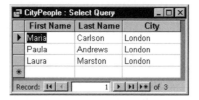

Type in a city ('london', for instance) and click OK.

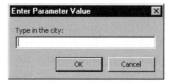

The answer table has located all records from your chosen city unless, of course, there are none.

❡ *In Chapter 4 we said that you can use wildcards to look for records when you aren't exactly sure what you're searching for. In a normal select query, if you type in car* as the criterion, Access converts this to:*

Like 'car*'

If you want to use a wildcard in a parameter query, simply create a parameter query that uses the LIKE operator and the wildcard symbol (*). For example:

Like [Enter the first letter to search by:] & "*"

will look for words that begin with a specified letter. While:

Like "*" & [Enter any letter to search by:] & "*"

will look for words that contain the specified letter. ❡

Creating a Range query

A range query locates records that fall within a specified range. A range can be time-based (between April 16 and August 19, or between 09:00 and 18:00) or value-based (between 30 and 100).

Again, you can start with a wizard-built select query and then modify it from the Design view to add a range criteria.

Range criteria use the Between...And operator. The syntax is just like English; we'd say 'Show me the records from between April 16 and August 19' and that's just how this operator works.

Examples of valid range criteria include:

Between 100 And 150
Between #01/01/60# And #31/12/62#
Between #08:30:00# And #12:20:00#

Records that meet the values that specify the starts and ends of ranges are included in the answer set. You can also use mathematical operators to the same effect, for instance, >=100 and <=150.

You can type in dates and times without the surrounding hashes and Access will add them automatically.

A typical range query might look like this

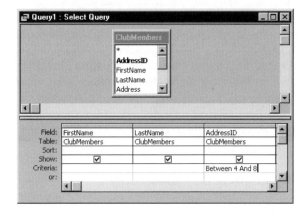

for finding records with address ID numbers between 4 and 8 inclusive.

Finally, we can combine Parameter and Range queries by using criteria like:

Between [Type the start date:] And [Type the end date:]

Creating Action queries

Action queries, as their name suggests, do things. They effect actual changes to the records in a table, either by deleting them, updating or adding new records (appending, in database-speak). A single query of any of these types can affect multiple records. Action queries are very powerful and are mainly used for database maintenance tasks.

- A delete query will delete from a table all records that match certain criteria. Delete queries always delete entire records, not just certain fields within records.
- An update query will locate records that match a criterion and then alter each record to contain the updated information.
- An append query is used to incorporate records from one table into another. Records from tables that contain different fields can be brought together with an append query.
- The fourth type of action query is the Make-Table query; we looked at this in Chapter 4. When the answer table produced by a query would be useful as a table in its own right, the Make-Table query does just that.

❦ *Action queries can accurately be called 'powerful' but remember that 'powerful' is also a euphemism for 'extremely, mind-bogglingly, dangerous'. A single delete query could, for example, remove all 200,000 customers from your table. Or one quick update query could turn the date of every order in the database to 1/1/2000; neither of these changes is likely to be helpful. We have no intention of trying to inhibit you from using these queries because when used carefully, they are almost magically effective. So please 'do do this at home' but equally importantly, please do any testing and development work using a copy of the database rather than the real thing. Then if something does goes wrong, you can recover painlessly. That is exactly what I do because no query designer gets everything right first time every time.* ❦

Creating a Delete query

You'd create a delete query if, for instance, the French club members started a break-away movement and formed their own independent club. A delete query could remove from the table all records for members based in France. Whether there was but one member in the table or 999 of them, the delete query would rout them all out and delete them.

This example will delete all the Seattle-based members from the `Club` database (nothing personal, Seattleites; it's just an example). Go to the Query tab in the database window and start the process of building a new query from Design view, based on the `ClubMembers` table. Click the arrow next to the Query Type icon and select Delete Query from the list (you may need to click the down arrow button at the bottom of the list to reveal the Delete Query option).

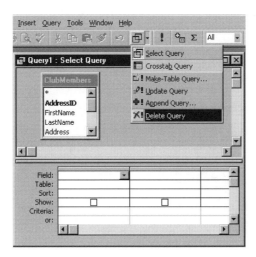

The title bar for the Design window now indicates that you're working on a delete query and the Query Design grid has acquired a row labeled Delete. Double click the asterisk from the `ClubMembers` field list: this step isn't compulsory but it will give you, in a few moments, a more comprehensive view of the records you're planning to delete. The Delete line now says 'From'.

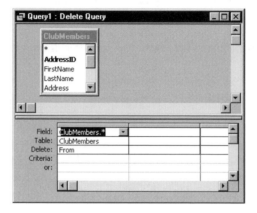

You have chosen the table from which you want records deleted, so now you set the criteria for the records to be deleted. Drag the City field from the list into the field row of the second column in the grid. The word 'Where' appears in the Delete row and in the criteria row below that, specify the records to be deleted. We're going to remove the details of people in Seattle, so type:

seattle

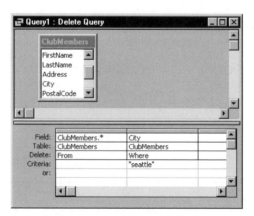

❛ *We said in Chapter 4 that when you're building queries, there is a difference between the Run button and the Datasheet view button. Here we'll see this difference in action.* ❜

Don't, at this point, click the Run button. Flip to the Datasheet view instead (using the first button in from the left on the toolbar) as this will show you the records that this query will delete *if* it is run. Showing all fields makes it easier to see what the query proposes to do to your data.

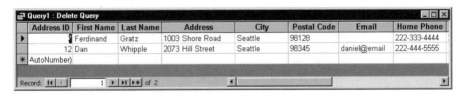

	Address ID	First Name	Last Name	Address	City	Postal Code	Email	Home Phone
▶	7	Ferdinand	Gratz	1003 Shore Road	Seattle	98128		222-333-4444
	12	Dan	Whipple	2073 Hill Street	Seattle	98345	daniel@email	222-444-5555
*	(AutoNumber)							

Record: ◄◄ ◄ 1 ► ►I ►* of 2

Click to return to Design view. This is the point at which, if you didn't see the records you expected, you'd edit the query accordingly, returning to the preview to check all is well.

When the records you want to delete are shown in the Datasheet view, return to the Design view one last time and actually run the query with a click on the Run button. A message window tells you that any rows deleted cannot be restored with the Undo button. Click Yes to continue. Look at the `ClubMembers` table: all the Seattle residents' records have, indeed, disappeared.

If you save this query as, say, `DeleteSeattleRecords`, add a Seattleite record to the table and then double click the query name, the query will warn you that it is about to delete records before running.

You can set criteria in more than one field, perhaps to identify those with email addresses who live in London (We're not sure why you'd want to persecute these individuals either, but the option's there).

The `chap9deletequery.mdb` contains the `DeleteSeattleRecords` query but it hasn't been run: you can do this and check the result. To return to a full set of member records, load up the `chap9start2.mdb`.

Creating an Update query

You would use an update query if you wanted to increase the sale price of your goods by 5%. The increase could either be applied to all items sold or just to those with a stock code beginning YSK. Similarly, if a supplier introduced a new coding structure which replaced YSK codes with JFX codes, you could bring your records into line with an update query.

So, as a demonstration, we'll assume that you've just discovered, much to your embarrassment, that you've spelled Kirkcaldy incorrectly in the addresses of all your friends living there. I've added two of these to the table, like this:

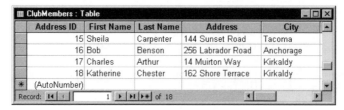

Address ID	First Name	Last Name	Address	City
15	Sheila	Carpenter	144 Sunset Road	Tacoma
16	Bob	Benson	256 Labrador Road	Anchorage
17	Charles	Arthur	14 Muirton Way	Kirkaldy
18	Katherine	Chester	162 Shore Terrace	Kirkaldy

For one or two records, you could easily make the change manually, but with a dozen or hundreds of records to update, you'd use an update query.

Start building a new query from the Design view, adding the `ClubMembers` table to the Table/Query pane. Click the Query Type icon and select Update Query from the list. The title bar for the Query Design window shows you're designing an update query and the design grid now contains an 'Update to' row. Add the `City` field to the Fields row and in the Criteria row type in the misspelling you want to locate, namely the records saying Kirkaldy in the `City` column.

In the Update To row in the same column, type in:

Kirkcaldy

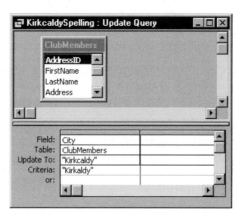

This will update the existing spelling with this new correct spelling, as you'll see when you run the query. (You can check that all is well by looking at the Datasheet view as before.) Exactly what you type in the Update To row will be written into the fields, so use capitals as required. A message window checks that it's OK to go ahead; click Yes if it is and the update query will run.

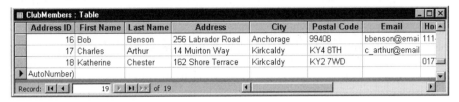

There, your street-cred is restored.

❢ *(Kirkcaldy is a charming town is Scotland, just north of Edinburgh, and is pronounced Kir-cod-ee rather than Kirk-aldy. I agree that you don't **need** to know this in order to run the query, but I thought the information might break up the heavy database stuff a bit. Kirkcaldy has a great Italian restaurant called La Gondola.)* ❢

Update queries can involve more than one field. For instance, you can locate the records for goods from Supplier X and increase the sum in the corresponding `Price` fields by 5%.

When you save a query, it appears in the list of queries (accessed by the Query tab) alongside an icon identifying the query type. If you can't identify a query type from the icon, highlight it and click the Properties button.

The `chap9updatequery.mdb` contains the `KirkcaldySpelling` query but it hasn't yet been run.

Creating an Append query

Append queries will add records from one table to another. For example, you decide to stock a new range of products and the manufacturer supplies an Access table detailing them. With an append query, you could add these records into your own ItemsStocked table automatically. This one's a real time-saver: imagine how much longer it would take to type in these new records and how many more errors would be likely to result if you did it manually.

This simple example of an append query will add records for three new members to the ClubMembers table in the Club database. The new records are held in a table called NewMembers: this table is included in the chap9start3.mdb.

Start with a new query in the Design view, adding the NewMembers table (the source of the new records) to the Table/Query pane. Click the Query Type icon and select Append Query from the list. A dialog asks for the name of the table to which you wish to append records (i.e. the destination of the new records); select ClubMembers from the pop down list and check the option button to indicate that it's in the current database. (You can also append to tables held elsewhere; just type in the file name and the path as necessary).

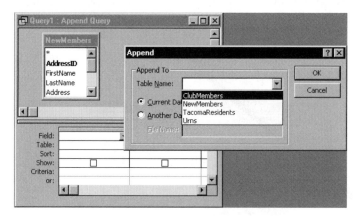

Click OK. At this point you determine which fields in the NewMembers table should be appended to the ClubMembers table. You should be aware that:

- if the source and destination tables both have AutoNumber fields you shouldn't add this field to the query. Access will automatically insert AutoNumber values into the destination table, giving records values leading on from the largest entry therein.

- if the field names in the source differ from those in the destination table, enter the field name used in the destination table into the query grid on the Append To row. In this case the asterisk cannot be used; each field must be entered individually into the grid.

I've selected everything but the AutoNumber `AddressID` field. Click into Datasheet view button to see the records that will be appended; return to Design view and run the append query. A message says this action will not be undo-able; click Yes to go ahead. Check out the `ClubMembers` table which now contains the new records.

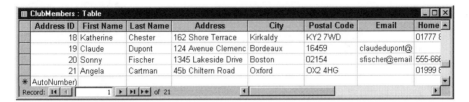

The query is saved as `AddNewMembers` and is present in the `chap9appendquery.mdb` file but it hasn't yet been run.

Creating a Group By query

In the table at the start of this chapter we listed Group By and Crosstab together because they do much the same sort of job. However, here we'll deal with them one at a time because they do differ in detail (and power).

Take a look at the `TreeOrders` table, shown below, from the `Tree` database in the `chap9start4.mdb` file.

SalesID	FirstName	LastName	Description	Price	Quantity
1	George	Thomas	Silver birch	$19.50	1
2	George	Thomas	Hornbeam	$17.00	2
3	Anna	Morgan	Hornbeam	$17.00	2
4	George	Thomas	Willow	$15.00	1
5	Jo	Green	Beech	$15.00	1
6	Jo	Green	Beech	$15.00	1
7	John	Parker	Ash	$15.00	1
8	Heather	Bell	Willow	$15.00	1
9	Anna	Morgan	Oak	$25.00	1
10	Heather	Bell	Oak	$25.00	1
11	John	Parker	Oak	$25.00	2

Record: 1 of 25

Create a new select query based on the `TreeOrders` table and showing three fields, `FirstName`, `LastName` and `Quantity`.

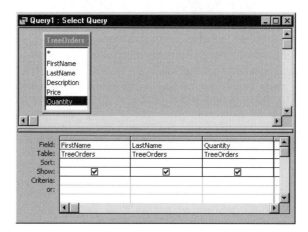

When you run it, you'll see, as expected, 25 records of which the first few are shown here:

FirstName	LastName	Quantity
George	Thomas	1
George	Thomas	2
Anna	Morgan	2
George	Thomas	1
Jo	Green	1
Jo	Green	1
John	Parker	1

Now, suppose that you want to see the total quantity for each person. In other words, you want to see each name only once in the answer table with the total beside it. Flip back to Design mode, locate the 'Totals' button in the toolbar

and press it. An extra row, labeled Total, appears in the lower part of the design window.

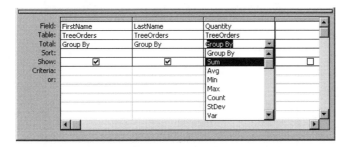

By default each field in this Total row reads 'Group By' but we want to change this, so click in this row under the Quantity field, then click the down arrow that appears.

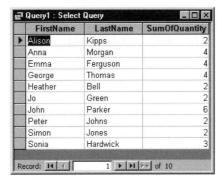

From the list select Sum and run the query.

FirstName	LastName	SumOfQuantity
Alison	Kipps	2
Anna	Morgan	4
Emma	Ferguson	4
George	Thomas	4
Heather	Bell	2
Jo	Green	2
John	Parker	6
Peter	Johns	2
Simon	Jones	2
Sonia	Hardwick	3

Record: 1 of 10

Magic. So how is it working? (It's saved under the name `GroupBy`.)

The Group By instruction under a field says 'find all of the records that have the same value in this field and put them together in the answer table.' The Sum instruction says 'add up the values found in this field for all of the records that have been put together by the Group By instruction.'

Ah, but you noticed that there were options other than Sum in there. Try selecting, say, Avg and re-running the query. You're way ahead of me; you guessed it would give the average. Have a play with the others while you're here.

Now try to answer this one before you try it. If you edit the original table so that Jo Green becomes John Green, what happens if we sum the quantities? After all, we already have a John Parker, so will the query show us the orders for these two individuals together?

The answer is...

FirstName	LastName	SumOfQuantity
Alison	Kipps	2
Anna	Morgan	4
Emma	Ferguson	4
George	Thomas	4
Heather	Bell	2
John	Green	2
John	Parker	6
Peter	Johns	2
Simon	Jones	2
Sonia	Hardwick	3

No, because we are grouping by two name fields, and both have to be the same before the records are put together. However, what would happen if we removed the `LastName` field from the query? Would the query then put all the 'John' records together? This is a more interesting question. After all, we know the records refer to different people, and, in a sense, Access 'knows' this as well because it has the data in the base table.

The answer is...

FirstName	SumOfQuantity
Alison	2
Anna	4
Emma	4
George	4
Heather	2
John	8
Peter	2
Simon	2
Sonia	3

that the John records **are** put together, which is an important point. A Group By query will group records on the basis of the fields that you choose for the query, not on the basis of the original records. In fact, once you think about it, this has to be the case. Each record in the original table has a different primary key value so if the value in every field in the base table was considered, no records could ever be grouped together.

Grouping is easy to demonstrate, but don't let that fool you: it's a very powerful tool. When you start to query databases in anger, it will be one of your best friends.

Creating a Crosstab query

A crosstab query is essentially a Group By query but with even more power. It is often the answer when you're juggling different ways of looking at a block of data, it adds an extra dimension to a Group By query and gives an answer table that is reminiscent of spreadsheet output. It lets you present data in two categories rather than one but with the same sum, average or whatever calculated for each intersection. This description, while accurate, probably doesn't mean too much and the easiest way to see what a crosstab does is to show you one.

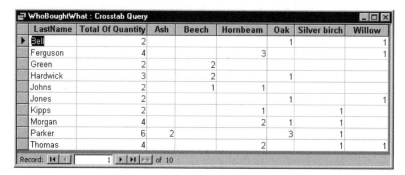

LastName	Total Of Quantity	Ash	Beech	Hornbeam	Oak	Silver birch	Willow
Bell	2				1		1
Ferguson	4			3			1
Green	2		2				
Hardwick	3		2		1		
Johns	2		1	1			
Jones	2				1		1
Kipps	2			1		1	
Morgan	4			2	1	1	
Parker	6	2			3	1	
Thomas	4			2		1	1

So that's an example of what a crosstab query can be induced to do; all you need to know is how to make it work. Just before we start, note that there are essentially three 'elements' in this crosstab. Down the left hand side are the last names of the people (taken from the LastName field in the original table) and these are acting as headings for the rows that we can see in the crosstab. Along the top are the names of the trees (from the Description field) which are acting as the headings of the columns. Finally, at the intersection of the rows and columns, there are the numbers of trees bought (Quantity field). In this crosstab, these numbers have been added (or summed) where appropriate. For example, John Parker has bought one oak and then another two and the crosstab shows the correct total of three at the intersection of Parker and Oak. In addition, he has bought two Ash trees and a Silver Birch, so his total for all trees is six.

Cross tabs can be created with a wizard, so the wizard is going to want to know:

1. which table you want to query;
2. which field to use for the row headings;
3. which field for the column headings;

4. which field for the intersections;

5. what mathematical operation (in this case, summing) to apply to the numbers at the intersections.

Right, armed with that foreknowledge, we'll build this query, starting with the Crosstab wizard.

In the Queries tab, click the New button from the top of the database window and select Crosstab Query Wizard. Select the `TreeOrders` table and click Next.

In this dialog you choose the row headings. Select the `LastName` field and it's illustrated in the sample display so you can check the orientation, as shown below.

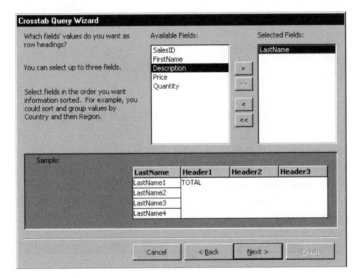

Click Next. Now select the field for the column headings – Description. Again your choice is illustrated by the sample. Click Next. This is where you determine the number you want to be calculated at the intersections, so select the Quantity field. Then select the Sum function. There is a check box for whether to include row sums: check it to include a total number of items purchased in the crosstab.

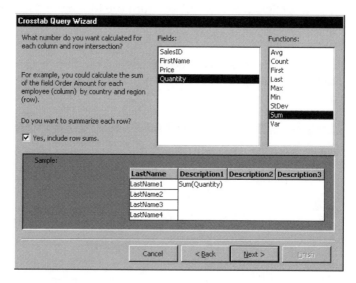

Click Next one more time, give your query a name (ours is WhoBoughtWhat), check that the option button for 'View the query' is selected and click Finish.

LastName	Total Of Quantity	Ash	Beech	Hornbeam	Oak	Silver birch	Willow
Bell	2				1		1
Ferguson	4			3			1
Green	2		2				
Hardwick	3		2		1		
Johns	2		1	1			
Jones	2				1		1
Kipps	2			1		1	
Morgan	4			2	1	1	
Parker	6	2			3	1	
Thomas	4			2		1	1

Record: 1 of 10

Easy!

It's worth having a look at the Design view of this crosstab query,

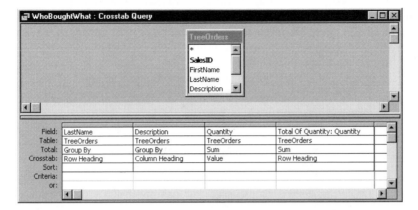

to get a feel for how it has been constructed. Once you get used to creating crosstabs, you can, of course, start tweaking in Design view to customize the query further. But for now, have a play and create some more crosstabs from this data.

The Crosstab wizard offers a range of functions apart from SUM, used above, and these are shown below.

Function	Description
AVG	Average of the values in a field
COUNT	Number of values in a field, not counting blank values
FIRST	Field value from the first record in the result set in a query
LAST	Field value from the last record in the result set in a query
MAX	Highest value in a field
MIN	Lowest value in a field
STDEV	Standard deviation of the values in a field
SUM	Totals the values in a field
VAR	Variance of the values in a field

We have taken some care to stress that a crosstab has three main elements because, unless you bear that in mind, sometimes you may get an answer that seems counter-intuitive. For example, John Parker has bought three oaks, all at $25 each. Suppose that when he bought two together we were generous and dropped the price to $20.

SalesID	FirstName	LastName	Description	Price	Quantity
25	John	Parker	Oak	$25.00	1
11	John	Parker	Oak	$20.00	2
19	John	Parker	Ash	$15.00	1
7	John	Parker	Ash	$15.00	1
12	John	Parker	Silver birch	$19.50	1
1	George	Thomas	Silver birch	$19.50	1
4	George	Thomas	Willow	$15.00	1
2	George	Thomas	Hornbeam	$17.00	2

TreeOrders : Table — Record: 23 of 25

The average price he has paid for oaks is now (20+20+25)/3 which is 65/3 which is $21.67. If you make the required change to the TreeOrders table and then create a crosstab query to show the average price, will it show $21.67 for Parker's oaks? At first thought this seems the obvious answer, but not if you think about the elements we give the cross tab in order to do the calculation. We tell it to look at the LastName, Description and Price fields. We haven't told it to look at the Quantity field at all, so it doesn't 'know' that John Parker bought two oaks at $20, it simply knows that there are two records for Parker buying oaks in the TreeOrders table – one gives the price as $25 and the other $20. The crosstab uses this data to calculate the averages, so in the answer it cites the average as $22.50.

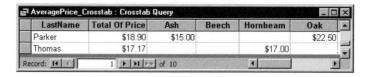

LastName	Total Of Price	Ash	Beech	Hornbeam	Oak
Parker	$18.90	$15.00			$22.50
Thomas	$17.17			$17.00	

AveragePrice_Crosstab : Crosstab Query — Record: 1 of 10

It is giving the right answer, based on the information we asked it to use. We aren't trying to make this out to be a big problem, it is just something that needs to be borne in mind. (This query is called AveragePrice_Crosstab).

Another point worth knowing is that you can create crosstab queries that use parameters. Here is one, called TreeChoice_Crosstab, all set to go.

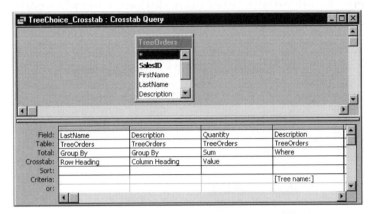

The only problem is that it won't run and instead generates an error message.

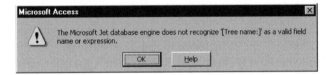

This is because, when you create a crosstab query that uses parameters, you have to tell Access the 'type' of data that is going to be used in the parameter. This is easy, all you have to do in Design view is to pop down the Query menu and select Parameters.

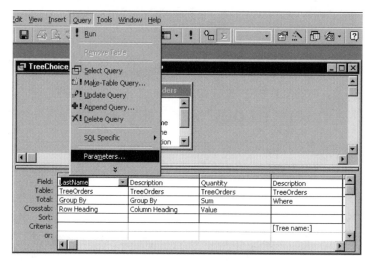

Then type in the same information as you typed into the Criteria line of the query and set the data type to text as shown here:

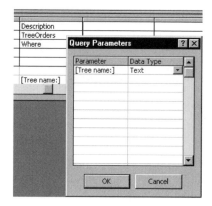

After that, the query should run like a normal parameter query.

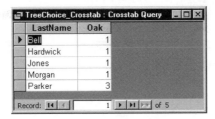

Using a query to perform calculations

Databases exist to enable the extraction of information from the data stored: that's the primary reason for building a database. Information like totals, averages and so on are really useful pieces of information but you don't usually store them in the database. The reason is simple. Take our table of tree sales. John Parker buys two oaks at $25 each, so I enter that information and the total, $50. When he comes to collect them I realize he is an old friend and change the price to $20 each. I amend the price per oak, but forget to amend the total. Six months later, I look at the record and see the anomaly but haven't a hope of remembering which value is incorrect – the price per oak, the number bought or the total. So, as a general rule we don't store totals, averages or any other data in a database that can be calculated (or derived) from the data that is already there. Instead we calculate it afresh whenever we need it and, as you've probably guessed, this can be done with queries.

We'll build the query which generates an answer table that totals the cost for each order.

The first step is to build a select query based on the `TreeOrders` table and using the four fields `LastName`, `Description`, `Quantity` and `Price`: use whichever method you prefer to get to this point. You want to add a new field for the total price that's to be calculated from the Price and Quantity fields. In Design view, in the Field row of a blank column type

```
TotalPrice: [Price]*[Quantity]
```

This says, in effect, 'create a field called `TotalPrice` and place in it values calculated by multiplying the value in the `Price` field by the value in the `Quantity` field'.

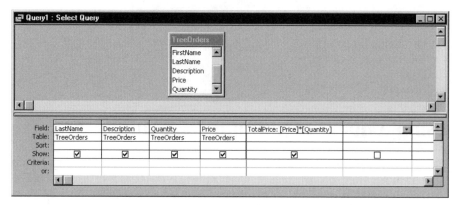

Click to Datasheet view to see the result.

LastName	Description	Price	Quantity	TotalPrice
Thomas	Silver birch	$19.50	1	$19.50
Thomas	Hornbeam	$17.00	2	$34.00
Morgan	Hornbeam	$17.00	2	$34.00
Thomas	Willow	$15.00	1	$15.00
Green	Beech	$15.00	1	$15.00
Green	Beech	$15.00	1	$15.00
Parker	Ash	$15.00	1	$15.00
Bell	Willow	$15.00	1	$15.00

Record: 1 of 25

I've saved this query as `PriceCalc`. Now if you edit the order for Parker to change the price per oak back to $25, you'll find that as soon as you move off the cell you've edited, the total automatically updates to the correct value before your very eyes!

LastName	Description	Price	Quantity	TotalPrice
Green	Beech	$15.00	1	$15.00
Parker	Ash	$15.00	1	$15.00
Bell	Willow	$15.00	1	$15.00
Morgan	Oak	$25.00	1	$25.00
Bell	Oak	$25.00	1	$25.00
Parker	Oak	$25.00	2	$50.00
Parker	Silver birch	$19.50	1	$19.50
Johns	Beech	$15.00	1	$15.00

Record: 11 of 25

You can now build a Crosstab query based on this query which will show, instead of the numbers of trees that have been purchased, the amount spent by each customer on each type of tree. Here it is in Design view

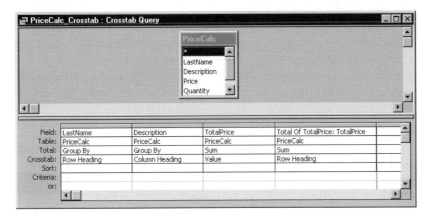

and in Datasheet view: it's called `PriceCalc_Crosstab`.

LastName	Total Of TotalPrice	Ash	Beech	Hornbeam	Oak	Silver birch	Willow
Bell	$40.00				$25.00		$15.00
Ferguson	$66.00			$51.00			$15.00
Green	$30.00		$30.00				
Hardwick	$55.00		$30.00		$25.00		
Johns	$32.00		$15.00	$17.00			
Jones	$40.00				$25.00		$15.00
Kipps	$36.50			$17.00		$19.50	
Morgan	$78.50			$34.00	$25.00	$19.50	
Parker	$124.50	$30.00			$75.00	$19.50	
Thomas	$68.50			$34.00		$19.50	$15.00

Record: 1 of 10

The `Tree` database with all these crosstab queries is in the `chap9crosstab.mdb` file.

Can you edit the data in an answer table?

You'll be familiar by now with the idea that data is stored in a table and also that queries produce tables. Tables for storing the raw data in a database are known as base tables while the ones generated by queries are called answer tables.

Answer tables and base tables share many attributes (see the section on closure later in this chapter); one of the few ways in which they can differ is whether you can edit the data they contain. Clearly you can edit the data in a base table but what about the data in an answer table? The answer is normally 'Yes' but you need to be aware that sometimes the answer is 'No'.

Imagine a select query that pulls out all the records for people living in Washington State and presents them in an answer table. You want to edit the address of a friend who has moved house; can you do that in the answer table? Yes, you can and the changes that you make in the answer table will appear in the base table upon which it is based.

Now consider the query above that has a calculated field called `TotalPrice`. The values in this field are generated from the values in `Price` and `Quantity` fields. Can you edit the total price values in this answer table? No, you can't (give it a try). The query has calculated the total price values from the values in two fields in the base table. If you alter the total price value for a record in the answer table, that alteration ought to be reflected in the base table. Which field should Access let you alter in the base table, the unit price or the quantity purchased? Access can't tell which alternative is the sensible one so in this case it will refuse to let you edit the answer table.

As a rule of thumb for establishing whether a field is editable or non-editable, consider what it is showing you. If it's simply a view of what's contained in the base table, you'll be able to make changes that will be incorporated into the underlying table. If some manipulation has been carried out on the fields you see in the answer table (the calculation of a sum, average or total, or the concatenation of text fields, for example) then you will not able to edit those fields. Please note, however, that this is only a rule of thumb. Sometimes answer tables are rendered un-editable for more complex reasons that fall outside the remit of this book. This shouldn't worry you too much because you can always simply try it. Build the query and try to edit the answer table. If Access allows you to perform the edit, then it considers the edit to be safe and you can go ahead.

Refining queries to home in more precisely upon records

Queries can be fine-tuned to help you find exactly the records for which you're searching; here are some of the more useful ways of performing this trick. We'll use the `ClubMembers` database again so if you wish to follow our steps, load up the `chap9start5.mdb` file.

For example, operators can be used in queries to help you home in on the records you want.

OR and AND

Two of the most commonly used operators are OR and AND: we met these in Chapter 4. Remember that using OR tends to increase the number of records in the answer table and that AND tends to decrease them.

LIKE

This works in a similar was to its English language equivalent: it's like saying 'Find me the address for that guy Jackson... or Johnson... whatever'. Such a query would look something like this:

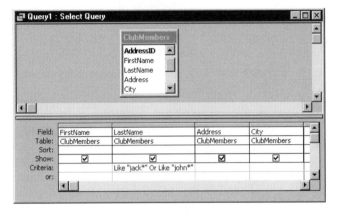

(You can simply type 'jack* or john*' and Access adds the inverted commas and both Likes).

The asterisks in this query are wildcards (see below); used in conjunction with these, LIKE is a very useful and powerful operator.

NOT

Another useful one, NOT. (No, it is, really it is). It can be thought of as the opposite of LIKE and lets you chop away the records you don't want on the occasions where that's easier than specifying the ones you do.

For instance, if you know that there are several people with the last name 'Dupont' in the database, and you know that you **don't** want the one who lives in Paris, you could use the following query:

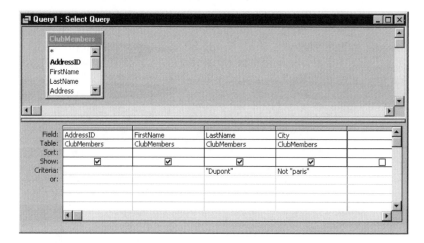

to further narrow the search.

BETWEEN...AND

We introduced this operator when we built a range query earlier in this chapter; it too works as it does in English syntax. Below is a typical example for finding a record in a specific range of dates:

Between #01/01/58# And #31/12/60#

Wildcards

A wildcard is a character that is used in place of an unknown character or characters. There are six, listed in the table below, of which * is the most commonly used.

Character	Action	Example
*	Matches any number of characters; can be first or last character in the search string	*pe* finds penguin & pencil; *pe* finds hope & calliope
?	Matches any single alphabetic character	?oad finds road, toad & load
[ ]	Matches any one of the characters within brackets	[rt]oad finds road & toad but not load
!	Matches any character not in the brackets	[!rt]oad finds load & goad but not road & toad
-	Matches any one of a range of characters; the range must be specified in ascending order (A to Z)	x[f-h]y finds xfy, xgy & xhy
#	Matches any single numeric character	4#5 finds 435, 405 & 465

The criterion

Like 'Jack*' Or Like 'John*'

used above says 'show me all the records where the value in the `LastName` field starts with the letters Jack or John with any and all combinations of letters after those'. Jackson and Johnsson are found, as would Jack, john, Jack789 and Johnstonely-Burlinghame if they had been in the table.

Display only the highest or lowest values in the query's results

It's also possible to restrict the scope of Select queries and of some Action queries with a query limiter called TopValue. As the name suggests this lets you find, for example, the top five selling products. Of course, 'Top' can refer to the lowest values in a list, so you can also find the eight worst performing sales people in your sales force...

The TopValues box

is accessible from the main menu when you have a query open in Design view. Entries can either be numbers (10, for instance, will give you the top ten records) or percentages (10% gives the top ten percent of records in the answer table).

For example, if you want to find the two tallest urns in your collection, the following will do it.

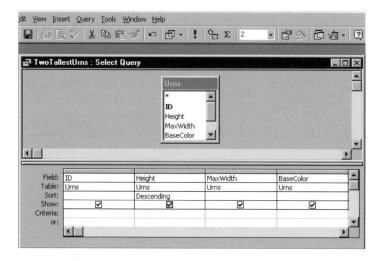

The field we want to use for the selection (Height) has been sorted into Descending order; in addition we have set the TopValues box to two. The answer table shows the result we want:

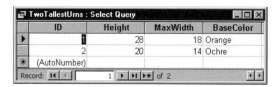

If we wanted the three smallest, we'd simply alter the query to this:

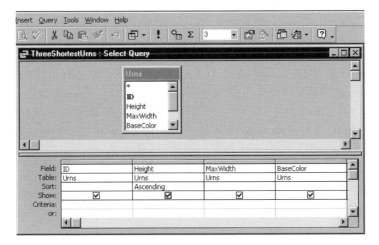

and the answer would be:

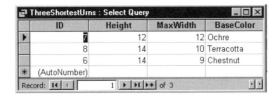

To make this a percentage rather than a number, simply followed the number in the TopValue box with a percent sign (%).

Closure – and making further use of queries

❛ *Closure is a term used in databases to describe the fact that answer tables not only look like but also behave like the underlying base tables. This is more important than it first appears...* ❜

Queries show you the data you want to see in an answer table. As you will have noticed by now, the answer tables that Access displays look very much like the base tables that hold the underlying data; both have rows and columns, both are editable (though see the exceptions discussed above in the section called 'Can you edit the data in an answer table?'). The fact that answer tables are constructed to look just like base tables is not accidental; it gives us much more flexibility in the ways in which we can manipulate the data in the database.

You know by now that you can build one or more forms on a base table in the same way that you can build one or more queries on a base table. Closure means that you can do exactly the same with answer tables that come from queries. That is to say, you can build forms that take their data from an answer table and you can build queries that take their data from an answer table.

Suppose that you have a massive customer table which holds all your customers from around the world. You create a query called `USACustomers` which extracts only the customers who live in the US. You can then build a form on that query called, perhaps, `American`. When you open up that form, the query will run automatically for you and in the form you will see only the US-based customers.

❢ *We should, in fact, say 'build a form on the answer table generated by that query' but common usage and a dislike of verbosity lead us to prefer the looser phrasing.* ❢

And/or you can build a query based upon `USACustomers` that shows the people who live in Seattle. You can go on and on. You could, for example, then build a form called, say, `SeattleCustomers` on **that** query. When you open that form, the first query runs, extracts the US customers and passes the answer table to the second query. That query extracts the Seattle customers and these are the ones you see in the form.

❢ *Warning: gratuitous plug approaching.*

This is all you need to know about closure in order to make use of it. If you end up interested in the background to closure and other aspects of the relational database model that Access uses, try Inside Relational Databases with examples in Access by Mark Whitehorn and Bill Marklyn, Springer-Verlag, ISBN 3-540-76092-X). ❢

We'll have a look at a couple of examples of where closure can be useful.

Using a query as the basis for a form

You spend a lot of time on the phone to club members and you're always looking up numbers. You create queries to divide members into those in the USA and those in Europe, showing the records in alphabetical order, but it's still a table to be looked through to find the right number. Base a form on this query and you can have a neat clean view of one record at a time and cycling through to the record you want is quick and easy. An example of such a form is shown below.

Start by building a select query to find all those resident in the USA: a field called `Country` has sidled into the `ClubMembers` table to make this possible. The query is called `USAPeople`. From the Form tab, start the Form wizard. Select the query from the Tables/Queries list, add all its fields, pick a layout (Columnar), a style (Stone) and a title (`USAPeoplePhoneNumbers`).

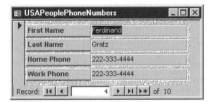

There it is, a friendly front-end to your list of contacts. This doesn't look quite like the one above; the layout and style are different and it lacks the customized image but it's perfectly usable and was created in a flash. (Changing the look of your forms is covered in Chapter 10).

As you work with your database, you'll find many more places where a form based on a query makes a whole lot of sense.

Using a query as the basis for a report

A report can be based on a query in the same way as a form can, and just as easily. You're going abroad and suspect that while you're away you'll need to make a few phone calls to keep things moving. It's the work of a moment to print out a list of contact details to slip into your suitcase.

In the Reports tab, start the Report wizard, select the underlying query (AllPhoneNumbers) and all its fields. Don't group the records, sort them by last name, use the Tabular layout, pick a style (Casual) and a name for the report (AllPhoneNumbers). Click Finish

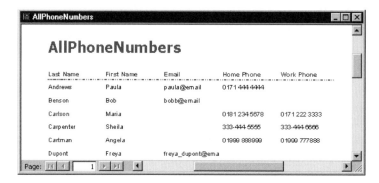

and there it is. Send it to the printer and you're heading for the airport in seconds flat.

The forms and report described above are in the file chap9end.mdb.

Using a query as the basis for another query

This sounds like weird recursive stuff. It is a bit, but it's also very useful. Imagine you have a query that identifies all the members in Europe. It's a useful query and you use it frequently. In time, the number of contacts grows to a point at which it is no longer efficient to flip through the records to find the information you want. The quickest way to find everyone you know in Paris who uses email is to build another query.

Rather than start again from the whole tableful of contacts, you can base the new query on the answer table generated by the original query. With a simple membership database this time saving may not be significant but with a vast table of thousands of orders, for instance, it could be a different story.

A query based on a query can be built manually or with the wizard. When you start the wizard, pop down the list of Tables/Queries and choose the query to base the new query upon. The manual method is just as simple. Click the Queries tab in the Show Table dialog and pick the one you want. The query can then be constructed just as if you were basing it on a table.

When you've completed the new query you simply run it: you don't have to run the query on which it is based. Access takes care of that; all you see is an answer table with the data requested.

Summary

Time and effort go into collecting data and filling a database with it. Queries are how you make your database work for you; they're the payoff once all the hard work has been done. Having put the data in, queries are how you get information out.

As we progress through the delights of querying, some of the examples may sound a little trivial. They are, but they're there to demonstrate the basic task that each type of query performs. Once you understand the principle of each, as your database grows you'll see more and more occasions when they can be pressed into service.

Combined with forms and reports, queries become even more powerful and flexible. Experimentation is the key: time spent playing with queries and their adjuncts is rarely wasted.

Chapter 10

Forms again – design

In Chapter 5 we looked at generating basic forms and then at how forms can be used to calculate values for you. In this chapter we're going to concentrate on using the form designer to customize forms further. However, we'll start by having a brief look at the other form wizards that Access offers and how these can be used.

If you opt to create a new form, Access offers a range of choices.

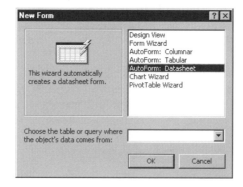

We've already used the Form wizard (Chapter 5), we'll be using Design in a moment and the three AutoForm options are so easy to use that we suggest that you simply run through each to see what it produces. The last two – Chart wizard and PivotTable wizard – are worth a slightly more detailed mention.

The Chart wizard

Give this one a try. In the `chap10start.mdb` file you'll find a tiny table called `Fish` so select it from the list of available tables and queries and click OK. In the next dialog, shown below, select both the fields

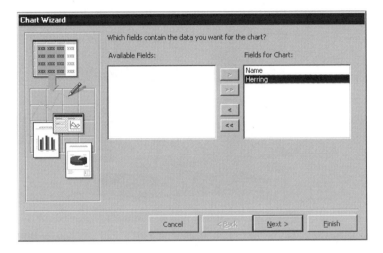

and press Next. The wizard will proceed to show you three more dialogs and by all means spend some time reading them though in each case the defaults happen to be fine. Finally, you will end up with a form which contains a graph.

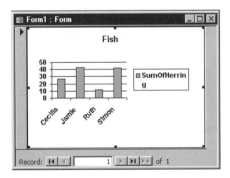

For Office users, this graph should look familiar because it is simply a Graph 2000 Chart. The good news is that Access uses this standard Office component, so if you are used to embedding graphs into, say, Word then you should find that from within Access it works in much the same way.

Since this book is about Access, rather than Office, we don't intend to spend much time on a standard Office component but at the risk of boring those who are familiar with Chart, it is worth making just a couple of points. If you right click on the chart you can get to see the properties as normal. However, from the right-click menu you can also select Chart Object, Open.

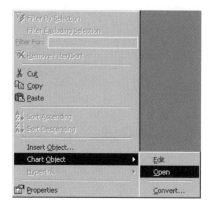

This will open up Microsoft Graph and if you right click on the chart in there,

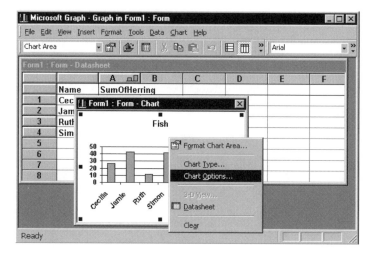

you can start to seriously tweak the chart.

The PivotTable wizard

This allows you to insert a Microsoft Excel Pivot Table into a form. (Note that this isn't going to work if Excel isn't installed on your machine!) Again, we don't intend to tell you everything there is to know about pivot tables, but showing you how to put one into a Access form seems eminently worthwhile.

Pivot tables come into their own when they are used with data from multi-table databases; in order to demonstrate their use here we have designed a table that would get zero marks for table design in a real database but serves our current purpose excellently. This table is called `Pivot` (it's in the `chap10start.mdb` file) and a sample of the data is shown here.

ID	City	Person	Item	Price	Number
1	London	Ross	Biscuits	$2.00	45
2	London	Sophie	Cigars	$50.00	5
3	London	Sophie	Beef Jerky	$12.00	3
4	Seattle	Ross	Biscuits	$5.00	12
5	Half Moon Bay	Katie	Toys	$35.00	3
6	London	Katie	Concert Tickets	$50.00	3
7	Seattle	Steve	Cigars	$50.00	2
8	Paris	Andrea	Toys	$23.00	4
9	Paris	Steve	Beef Jerky	$12.00	4

So click on New, choose the PivotTable wizard and select the Pivot table. The first dialog simply tells you what a pivot table is, so click on Next and select the four fields shown

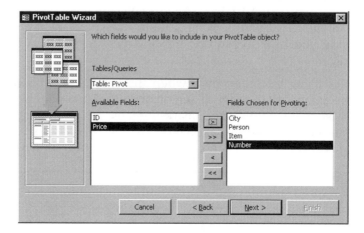

and press Next.

Excel should open up (because the pivot table is not only going to be created in Excel but controlled thereafter by Excel) and this dialog appears.

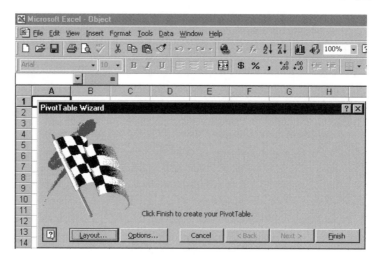

Click on Layout and use the mouse to drag and drop the field buttons as shown below. (When you drop the number field onto the Data area it will automatically change to 'Sum of Number').

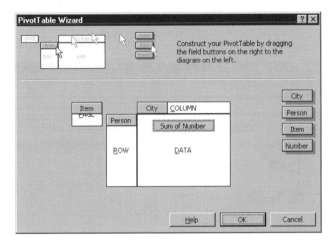

Click on OK and then on the Finish button in the underlying dialog, whereupon you should pop back to Access and the form should appear. Some re-sizing in Design view may be necessary at this point to enable you to see all of the data.

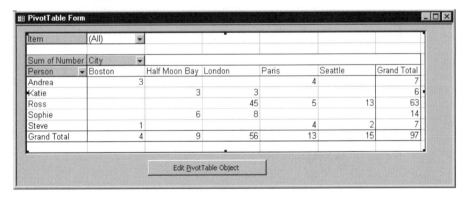

Sum of Number	City					
Person	Boston	Half Moon Bay	London	Paris	Seattle	Grand Total
Andrea	3				4	7
Katie		3	3			6
Ross			45	5	13	63
Sophie		6	8			14
Steve	1			4	2	7
Grand Total	4	9	56	13	15	97

Save the form as `PivotTableForm` and we can start to see how it works. The pivot table shows the cities along the top of the grid and the people down the left hand side. It is summarizing the values from the Number field at the intersections of those labels. Thus Sophie has bought a total of eight items in London so that value is shown in the intersection of Sophie and London.

One of the great joys of a pivot table is that it is highly versatile. So we can, for example, get it to show us just the values for a particular item rather than for all items. Double click on pivot table in the form (or click on the 'Edit Pivot Table Object' button) and Excel should re-open. Pop down the Data menu in Excel and select 'Refresh data'. Then, click on All and select Toys

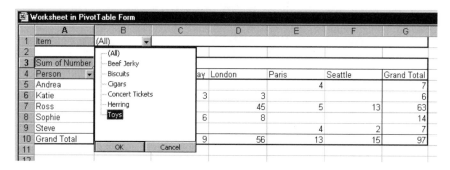

and then press OK.

This updates the pivot table in Excel and when you close Excel, you should find the pivot table in the form has updated.

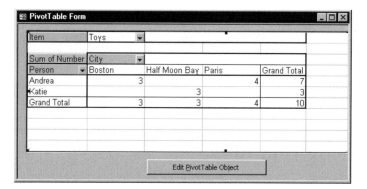

Double click on the pivot table again to go into Excel once more. Select Data, Refresh Data and then move the components of the pivot table around by dragging and dropping.

	A	B	C
1			
2	City	London	
3			
4	Sum of Number		
5	Person	Item	Total
6	Katie	Concert Tickets	3
7	Katie Total		3
8	Ross	Biscuits	45
9	Ross Total		45
10	Sophie	Beef Jerky	3
11		Cigars	5
12	Sophie Total		8
13	Grand Total		56
14			
15			

Worksheet in PivotTable Form

Try adding some more data to the Pivot table (the underlying table called Pivot, that is) and then re-opening the form. Unusually for a form, it won't automatically show the new data; you have to double click on the pivot table and select Data, Refresh Data in the Excel menu system, or click this button

on the PivotTable toolbox.

Pivot tables are powerful and great fun to use.

Designing your form

Forms are the face your Access database presents to the world. Even if you are the sole user of the database they are useful. However, when you start to build databases for other people to use, people who may be less computer literate than you, they become invaluable. An uncluttered form in cool colors that shows the fields you need is more conducive to accurate data entry than one looking like a dog's dinner.

You're given control over a form's appearance in Design view. Use the wizard to create a form showing all fields in the ClubMembers table. Use the columnar layout, the standard style, and call the result PlainForm.

Flip into the Design view (or, on the last page of the wizard, select the 'Modify the form's design' option).

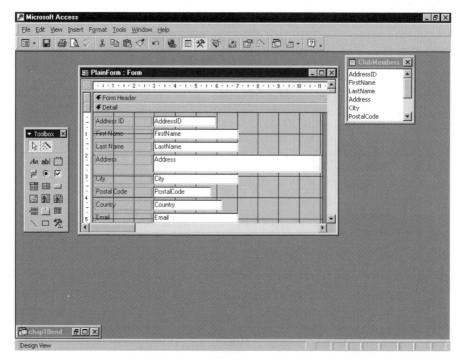

❦ *It's an oddity that if you select 'Modify the form's design' option, when the form opens in Design view, it has the default name of* Form1 *in its title bar, rather than the name you specified to the wizard. When you close the form, however, it's saved by your chosen name, so Access does know what's going on really...* ❧

This is your design environment. The toolbox is shown in this screen shot; if it isn't visible on your screen, click on the toolbox icon in the Form Design toolbar. The Field List is open too, showing the fields in the table on which the form is based; if it isn't open, click the Field List button.

The form has two gray bands at the top labeled Form Header and Detail, and one at the bottom called Form Footer. (If you can't see the Form Footer band, drag to make the window bigger until you can). The footer and header sections are not in use at present. Below the Detail band is an area covered by a grid, known as the Detail section.

Moving fields

Make some room on the form by placing the cursor on the bottom right corner of the Detail section and when the cursor turns into a four-headed arrow, drag the corner in a south-easterly direction.

Each field is represented by two parts. To the left is a Label that identifies the contents of the field. The label is transparent and its text appears on top of the form's background (flip to Form view to check this). To the right is a Text box where the data from the field is displayed. This defaults to a sunken white box in Form view.

Click anywhere in a text box and handles will appear around the text box and also around the associated label. Mostly you'll want to move these two together, so aim the cursor at the edge of the text box until it shows as an open hand. Now click and drag to move text box and label together to a new position.

To move a text box independently, put the cursor on its top left corner whereupon it shows as a pointing hand. Click and drag to move it without the label coming too. This technique works for moving labels too.

You can also select a batch of fields and labels in order to move (or otherwise manipulate) them all at once. Click somewhere on the gridded area and drag a rubber band outline to encompass, or at least to pass through, all the objects you want to select. When you release the button, handles appear on all the objects and they can be moved just as you move any single object.

Deleting fields

To delete a text box and label, click on the text box and press the Delete key. To remove a label and leave the text box, click on the label and press Delete.

Inserting fields

If you don't have the Field List on screen, click the Field List button in the main button bar or click View, Field List. You can drag this list of fields to anywhere on screen. To insert a field, click and drag a field name from the list onto the form.

Changing the tab order of fields

When in Form view, pressing the Tab key moves you from field to field in a certain order. This sequence is known as a form's 'tab order'. In the PlainForm form, this is the order in which the fields appear in the under-lying table. Usually the default tab order is fine but if you move fields around the form, that default may no longer seem so logical.

To inspect the tab order, flip into Design view, click View from the main menu and Tab Order... (If it isn't shown as an option, expand the list).

As the dialog explains, you can highlight each field name and drag it up or down the list to create the order you want. Click on the grey square to the left of each field name to select and move it by dragging. The Auto Order button is useful for reinstating the default tab order. Click OK when the order is to your liking.

❦ *You can also right click anywhere on the form and select the Tab Order option from the pop out menu.* ❧

Formatting your form with colors and fonts

Using color isn't necessary or obligatory, but it often improves the look of a form and gives you and any other users a more attractive workplace.

To change the background color, right click on the Detail section of the form, highlight the Fill/Back Color option and chose the color you want from the pop out palette.

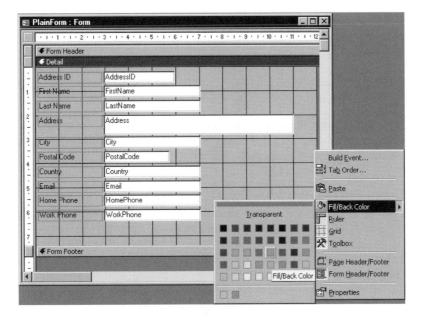

Sometimes it is easier to see the effect of these changes in Form view rather than in Design view. Access 2000 allows you to view the properties and to change some of them even when not in Design view. To demonstrate this, change to Form view. Make sure that the Formatting (Form/Report) toolbar is visible – if not, right click on the existing tool bar and select the formatting one.

Then call up the properties box by clicking on the Properties button in the Form Design toolbar. Now click on the Detail section of the form and the heading of the properties box will change to read Section Detail. Now you can use the Fill/Back Color button

in the Formatting toolbar to change the color of the section or of any other object that you select.

Sadly we aren't able to have color pictures to illustrate the excesses that can be wrought by changing this background color and the color properties of all the other objects. (You can set the Back Color, Fore Color and Border Color for each text box alone...)

Fonts are changed equally easily. With a label or text box selected, inspect the Font Name and Font Size properties on the Format tab. Both have pop down lists to let you change fonts and sizes. As you can see, Access allows you to make these formatting changes in a host of different ways – from both the Design and Form views, and from the toolbars or from the property box itself.

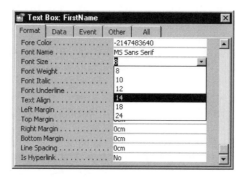

However, some of the design work can only be done in the Design view so it is best to work there for the rest of the chapter.

Changing field lengths and widths

You may decide that you need labels and text boxes to be bigger. This is often the case if you change fonts and/or font sizes, as described above. If I change the font size of the First Name text box to 18 and flip to Form view, the entry in the field is now so large that it's illegible on the form.

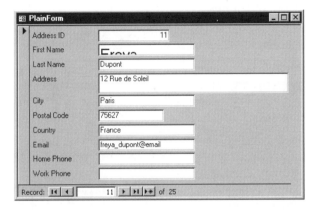

To make a text box bigger, select it with a click and then place the cursor on one of its sides. When the cursor shows a double headed arrow, you can drag to enlarge the box. Placing the cursor on a top right, lower right or lower left corner to show a slanting double headed arrow lets you drag to change the width and height simultaneously. Labels can be resized in the same way.

Adding graphics to your form

You can add graphics to your forms for fun or to give them a professional appearance. If you have a company logo stored electronically, you can put it on forms for a co-ordinated look. There is a ton of clip art around these days to cover the fun angle.

From the Toolbox, click on the Image tool.

Click on your form and drag an outline to be filled by the graphic. When you release the mouse button, a window for navigating to the chosen image appears: a preview of most graphics is shown on screen to help you choose. Do this and click OK when you've found one.

165

Sometimes, depending on the provenance of the graphics file, the box outlined will only show a small section of an image that's much too large to fit and sometimes it will look completely blank, both in Design and Form view.

Look at the properties for the Image and set the Size Mode (found under Format) to Zoom. The image should now appear in the Image box and be scaled to fit inside its outline.

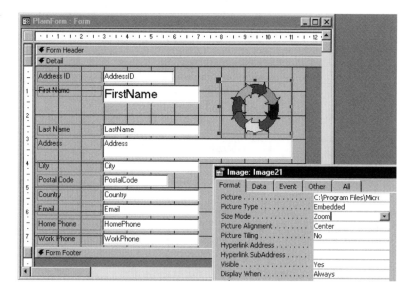

If you resize the image box on the form, the image itself will continue to zoom to fill the space you've given it. Borders can be put around an illustration: check out the Border Style, Color and Width properties.

Headers and Footers

To include a header on your form, put the cursor on the top of the Detail band so that it shows as a horizontal bar with a two-headed arrow through it. Now click and drag downwards and a new gridded area appears under the Form Header band. Here you can add a label with a title for the form, a graphic or whatever you want at the top of the form.

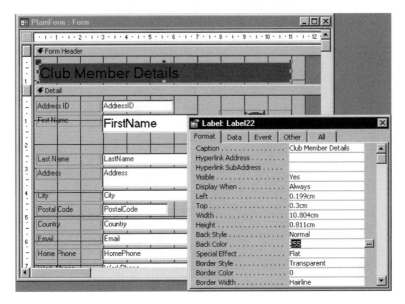

In Form view, any objects in the header will remain on screen, even if your form becomes so long that it fills more than one computer screen.

The Form Footer works in just the same way (drag the lower edge of its band to pull out a working area) and anything placed here will be visible as you inspect records.

Summary

Changing the appearance of your forms and jazzing them up with colors, fonts and graphics is enormous fun.

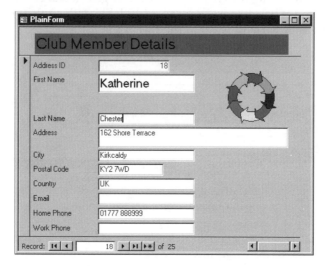

It's also good practice for manipulating objects and setting properties, so we really recommend that you spend some time experimenting at this point. But beware: don't go too mad with your works of art. Excessive jazziness often looks untidy and unprofessional, an impression you're unlikely to want to give, especially for forms to be used by others. Restraint is the key.

The file `chap10end.mdb` contains the three forms created in this chapter: PivotTableForm, PlainForm and NotSoPlainForm (this last is a somewhat tweaked version of PlainForm).

Chapter 11

Forms again – controlling data entry

Data validation

Time that you spend ensuring that only sensible data gets into your database is almost always time well spent. The motivation for collecting data and storing it in a database is that you want to extract it later, to find specific information, to see if any trends develop, to find any unexpected overlaps or omissions. The information you hope to take out can only ever be as accurate as the data that's entered so data validation at the point of entry for new records is crucial.

This topic has already been mentioned in Chapter 8 and various methods of controlling data entry were covered. However, these were all implemented from the Design view of the table destined to contain the data. Further data validation methods are available in Access's armory and can be put onto a form in Design view.

A tiny bit of theory

This book is aimed at getting you up and running with Access as quickly as possible. You may, however, be wondering why Access provides two very different places where data entry can be controlled – the table and the form. Well, flexibility is the trite answer, but it's an unhelpful one unless you know why such flexibility is useful. Think of it this way. You can have many different forms and queries based on a table. If you put a control on how data is entered into a table, then that control will automatically be applied to every form and query that uses that table. No new form or query will be allowed to subvert the rule. However, if you place the control on a form then that control applies only to data entered using that form. In other words, controls placed on tables are more all-encompassing, more powerful. There are times when that power is very useful (when a control needs to be rigorously applied to the data), and times when it is unhelpful (when the control needs to be applied sparingly). The choice is yours, which is where the flexibility comes in.

Form controls introduced

Form controls are objects that sit on forms to display records, perform actions or make it easier for people to use the form. There are different types of control, as discussed below, but they can all help you determine what can and can't go into the database by their actions or by pointing the way. Some controls are passive – labels, for instance, just sit there providing helpful information to the user of the form. Some are active, for example, only letting predetermined entries into a field (as does the Lookup Wizard data type mentioned in Chapter 8).

The best way to see how they work is to build some, so that's what we'll do – build a form that contains all of the elements described in the chapter. Clearly this is going to lead to a cluttered, complex form – exactly the sort that we would normally recommend that you try to avoid creating. However, we hope that you will forgive the excesses and appreciate that this is just an example of what you **can** do, not of what you **should** do.

Bound, unbound and calculated controls

Controls come in three flavors, bound, unbound and calculated. A bound control is tied (or bound, hence the name) to a field in an underlying table or query and this underlying field is the data source for the control. A bound control is used to display existing data from a field in the underlying table for inspection, editing and for entering new data.

An unbound control doesn't have a data source. Unbound controls are used to display messages, lines, rectangles and pictures that help users navigate and use the form.

A calculated control has an expression as its source of data. The expression can manipulate data from a field or fields in the underlying table or from another control on the form. Calculated controls are useful for showing information that's helpful for users of the form but not sensible to store in the table because it can be derived easily.

❛ *As we did when discussing queries, we are keen to convince you that storing derivable data in a table is usually a bad idea. Just as queries can be used to calculate derivable data when you need it, so can forms.* ❜

Overview of controlling form controls

Adding a form control

To place a control onto a form, you must be in Design view with the Toolbox open.

❛ *When you're starting to work with controls, it's helpful to make the Control wizards available by clicking the button at the top of the Toolbox. This will activate a wizard for some of the more complex controls when you place them on the form.* ❜

Select the control from the Toolbox by clicking on it. Move the cursor over to the form. If you just click on the form a control of default size will appear. Or you can click and drag to outline the shape and size of the control you want; as this can be altered later, pinpoint accuracy isn't needed at this stage. On releasing the mouse button, the control appears in place on the form, or a wizard runs to help you to build it. Once it's complete, flip to Form view to see the result.

Deleting a form control

In Design view, click on a control so that its handles appear and press the Delete key. Elements of some controls can be deleted separately: the label alongside an option button or check box can be removed, leaving the button itself, by clicking on the label and pressing Delete.

Moving a form control

Click anywhere on a control so that its handles appear. Aim the cursor at one edge until it shows as an open hand then click and drag to move it. Elements of controls can be moved independently by aiming the cursor at the top left corner of the element to be moved. When the cursor looks like a pointing hand, click and drag the element to its new position.

Sizing a form control

To change the size of a control, select it by clicking and place the cursor on one of its sides. When the cursor shows a double headed arrow, drag to enlarge or reduce the control's size. Placing the cursor on a corner so it shows a slanting double headed arrow lets you drag to change the width and height simultaneously.

Formatting controls

Most controls have formatting properties; these are listed on the Format tab of the Property list. You can change the Back Color of an option group, give an option button a sunken Special Effect and so on by clicking to select the object in question and editing its properties in the Property list.

Selecting multiple controls for editing/formatting

There are two ways to select multiple controls for batch editing or formatting.

Click on one object then, with the Shift key pressed, click on the other objects you wish to select. When they all have handles, proceed with the changes.

Alternatively you can start from anywhere on the Detail section background and click and drag to pull out a rectangle to encompass (or at least pass through) any object you wish to select. When they all have handles, changes can be implemented.

Controls in use

OK, that was the overview and now we're going to start with a blank form and add a number of controls, but bear in mind that when you use these controls for real, there is absolutely nothing to stop you adding them to a

form which has been generated with a wizard. Open up the
`chap11start.mdb` file, select the Forms tab and click on the New button.
In the dialog that appears, click on Design View and select the
`ClubMembers` table.

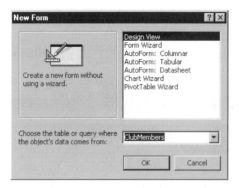

A new form appears, a blank canvas upon which you can work your magic.
Make sure that the toolbox, properties box and field list are all open. Click
on the format tab of the properties box.

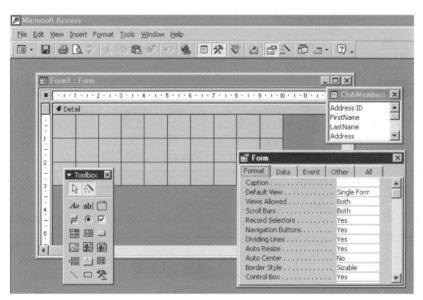

Types of form control

Label

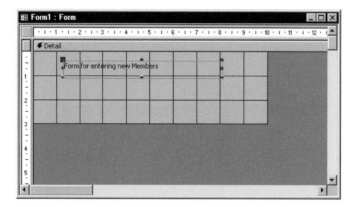

Put a label on the top of the blank form, type in some text and press the Enter key.

The Caption property of the Label shows as the text you have just typed in. We aren't going to keep on telling you to look at the properties of the controls you create because that will get boring, but we do recommend that you keep referring to them throughout this exercise because it will give you a feel for the parameters you can set for each control. As an example, have a look at the property called 'Display When' for the Label. Its possible states are Always, Print Only and Screen Only. These are ideal for messages to users that you don't want to appear on printed output, or vice versa. You can also use the properties box to set the font size, color etc., and/or you can do this using the tools in the formatting toolbar at the top of the screen. (If you can't see this toolbar, right click on the menu bar and select it from the list).

Labels can say anything you want then to. So, for example, you might find that users were continually trying to enter dates in DD/MM/YYYY format, when your database was expecting MM/DD/YYYY. You could add a label next to the date text box saying: 'Please enter dates with the month first, then the day and finally all four digits of the year – for example, 05/23/2002.'

Combo Box

Combo boxes are great for entering data into fields where only a limited range of values is likely. For example, entries in the `Title` column of the `ClubMembers` table are likely be mainly Ms, Miss, Mrs and Mr entries with a scattering of Dr, Prof and Rev entries and maybe some in different languages, like Mme or Herr. Users of your form can be presented with a list of the commonest titles for ease of selection and still have the option of typing in rarer ones. Or alternatively, you can force the user to use only the options that appear in the combo box. It's up to you, and, once the combo box is complete, you can swap it between these two behaviors by changing the 'Limit to List' property.

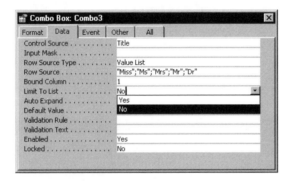

❦ *During the course of this chapter, you'll notice that fields appear in the ClubMembers table without so much as a by-your-leave, like the Title field referred to above. Don't worry about this, it's simply so that we have data to hand for illustrating various types of control.* ❦

To create a `Title` combo box, place a Combo Box control on the form and the Combo Box wizard opens.

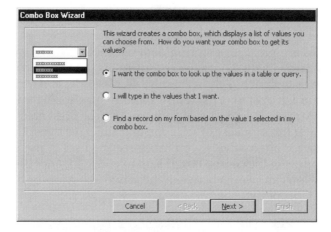

Click the middle button to type your own values and in the next step, leave the number of columns as one and start entering a title into the first cell. Fill in the entries you want (making sure the last one has been posted by clicking in the gray cell to remove the editing pencil)

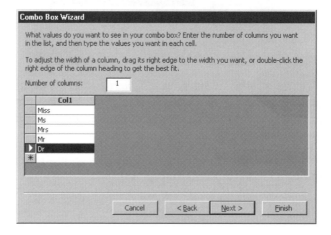

and click Next. Now click the 'Store that value...' option and select the Title field.

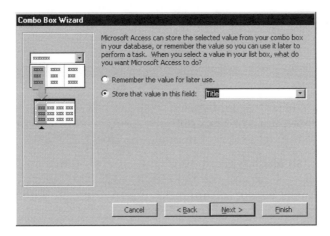

Finally, label the combo box and the process is complete. This is how the control will appear to users: a click on the arrowhead displays the list ready for a selection to be made.

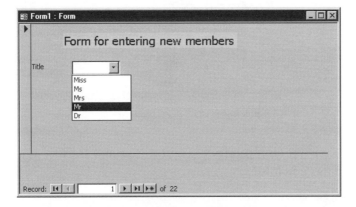

Although highly useful in this instance, combo boxes really come into their own when used in a database with more than one table so we'll revisit this useful control in a later chapter (Chapter 18).

Text Box

ab|

Text boxes are most frequently used to show the contents of a field in the underlying table. Put a text box onto the form, making sure that you position it over to the right to accommodate the label to the left.

A newly-created text box is unbound; the Control Source property (under the Data tab) is blank and the field itself reads 'Unbound'. Click to pop down the Control Source list and pick a field to associate with the text box: we're using `FirstName`.

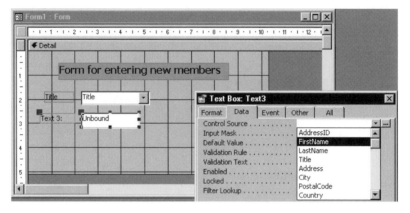

You now have a bound text box. You can also alter the text of the label to something more helpful.

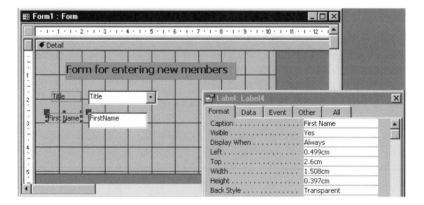

As well as the tool and property boxes, a list of the fields in the table with which you're working is also shown in Design view.

This offers a quick way of adding text boxes to a form. Click and drag a field from this list to place it and its label on the form. Text boxes adding in this way are automatically bound to the field in the underlying table. Add a text box for data from the LastName field using this method.

'Text box' is a slightly misleading term since it implies that only text can be displayed; in fact, text boxes can display numerical information and can also be used to perform calculations. Just to show how it is done, we'll create a text box that performs a 'calculation' on some text.

Now might be a good time to save your new form. Thus far, Access has referred to it by the default name of Form1 so click the Save button and type a name when prompted. Our example is called ClutteredForm because by the end of the chapter that's how it will look.

Then add another text box and, instead of binding it directly to a field, click on the ellipse button which appears at the end of the Control Source property.

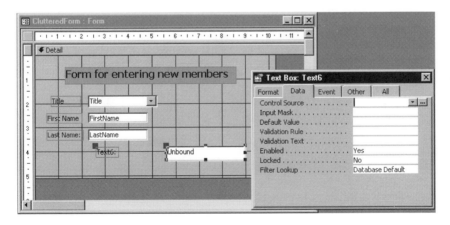

This opens the Expression builder. In the left pane select ClutteredForm, in the middle pane choose Field List and double click on Title in the right hand pane.

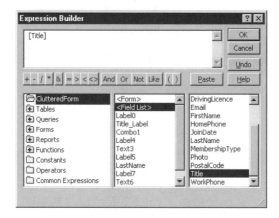

The formula we are going to build is:

```
[Title]+" "+[FirstName]+" "+[LastName]
```

which is easiest to build using a mixture of the keyboard and options selected from the expression builder.

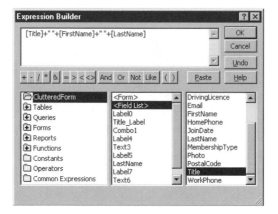

When it's complete, click on the OK button and this formula appears as the control source (plus a leading equals sign that Access has added).

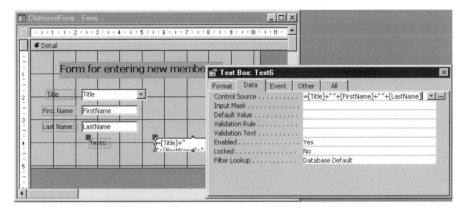

Change the label for the text box to something like Full Name and then test it. It should simply add (or concatenate) the three text fields into one.

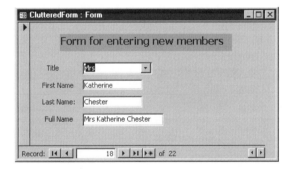

Toggle Button, Option Button and Check Box

These three work in much the same way: the main difference between them is how they appear on the form so we'll describe how to create and use a Check box and leave you to experiment with the others.

A check box button can be bound to a Yes/No field. We're about to bind a check box to a Yes/No field called DrivingLicence. Once it is in place on the form, clicking on the check box (or on its label) toggles it between two states – checked and unchecked. A check mark indicates Yes and unchecked No. When existing records are inspected, the toggle button reflects the entry in the field, appearing to have been selected if a licence is held and vice versa.

So, put a check box control on the form, set the Control Source to be the field DrivingLicence and amend the label accordingly.

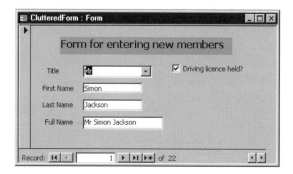

Just for fun, we've added a toggle button and an option button and bound all three to the same `DrivingLicence` field. An option button doesn't automatically come with a label so you can choose whether to add one or to enlarge the button sufficiently to take a suitable caption as we've done here.

We would never suggest, even for a moment, that binding more than one of these controls to the same field was sensible for a real form, but it does allow you to play with all three.

Option Group

OK, this is where we start to work with the more complex controls that really let you create powerful forms. Suppose you want to collect information which is more complex than Yes/No – perhaps you offer different types of club membership – Gold, Silver and Bronze. You could simply provide a text box on the form but this solution gives people entering the data no information about the available options. It is much better to provide a control to guide them and which, at the same time, only allows them to select a viable option.

An option group is a control that contains other controls of the toggle button, option button or check box type. Its purpose is to allow users to make a single selection from a group of two or more items with each item labeled.

Each option in the group is given by default an arbitrary value (though you can change these) and when an option is selected by the user of the form, the option's value is stored in a field in the underlying table.

In fact, the value doesn't have to be stored in the table, it can be stored by Access for later use. However, this 'later use' bit is only likely to be useful when you start to use Access' built-in programming language so it can safely be ignored for now.

I've added a field to the `ClubMembers` table to contain the type of membership. An option group to select the membership type can be placed on any form based on that table. Open `ClutteredForm` in Design mode, click the Option Group button and drag an outline onto the form. This runs the Option Group Wizard. In the first step you label the options.

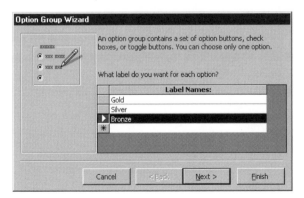

Click Next and in the second step you decide whether to set one of them as the default; this is usually the option that's chosen most frequently.

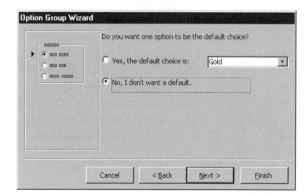

The next step shows the values that are assigned to each option: alter them if you wish but in this case, the values look entirely reasonable – 1 will represent Gold, 2 Silver and 3 Bronze.

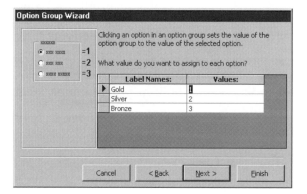

Next you determine what happens to the choice made by the user. As discussed above, the value is normally stored in a field which can be chosen
from a pop down list. Here I've selected the `MembershipType` field.

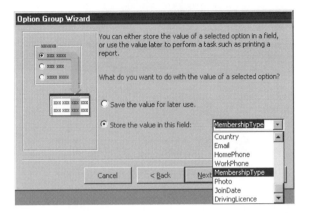

Choose the type of control in the next step and the style of display

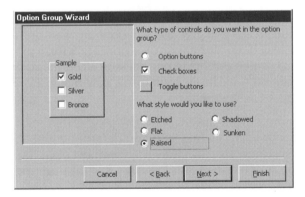

and in the final step, give the option group a caption before clicking Finish.

The completed option group looks like this in Form view:

Command Button

A command button lets you give users the option of issuing a command to Access. Actions such as saving a record, printing a form or moving to the previous record can be performed by clicking a command button. Placing buttons for common tasks on your forms can make those forms much easier to use, so let's experiment.

Place a command button onto ClutteredForm: this activates the Command Button wizard. In its first step you determine what the button will do. There are six categories of action, each with between four and eight actions. Here I've selected the Goto Previous Record from the Record Navigation category.

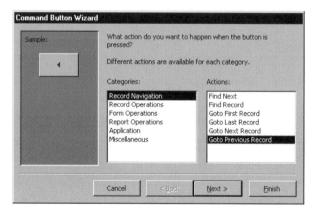

In the second step you can decide whether to display text or an icon on the button.

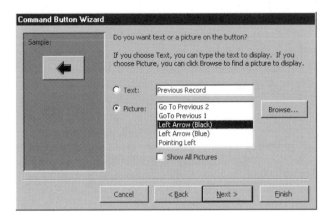

● *Checking Show All Pictures gives a much larger range of icons, including:*

and

'

Finally, give a name to the command button like `GoBackOneRecord`. This name isn't shown on the form but is shown under the Other tab in the Properties list.

Try out the button in Form view: it works just as you'd expect, even coming up with an error message 'You can't go to the specified record' if you click it when inspecting the first record.

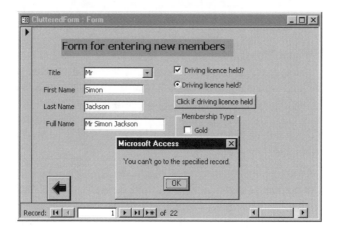

Line and Rectangle

These controls let you place lines and rectangles on your forms. Though simple, these can be used to group fields and controls and generally lead the eye of the user. Try changing a line's Border Style, Color and Width properties to add emphasis.

Image

With this sort of control, images can be put onto forms. Images can be anything from output generated with a painting package to off-the-shelf clip art. Placing an image control onto a form was covered in Chapter 10.

More Controls

Wow! Clicking this icon produces a vast list of weird and wonderful controls, some available and some not. The extent of this list is an indication of how important Access controls have become since the product first appeared. Whilst some of these extras come from Microsoft itself, many more come from third party suppliers, all of whom think it worthwhile to create specialist controls for Access users. Furthermore, this list is far from exhaustive: even more controls can be bought and/or downloaded from the Internet.

We can't possibly cover all these controls here so we'll select one to look at in some detail and leave further investigation to you. We've chosen Calendar Control 9.0 because the handling of dates can be a pain in the neck and this control does a great job of keep things in order.

Click the More Controls icon and select Calendar Control.

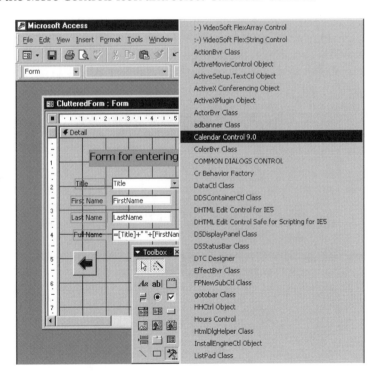

Drag to outline a large area on the form: about 5 × 7 cm (2 × 3 inches) is not unreasonable. When you release the mouse, a calendar appears, looking like this:

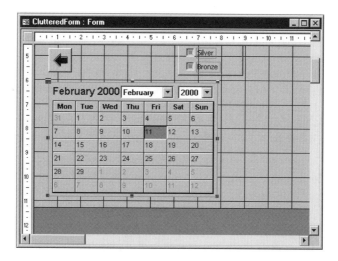

This gives users a familiar way in which to enter dates: the month and year can be selected from lists if the date isn't in the current month and then the day selected by clicking on the appropriate cell in the calendar. Here it is in use with a label added to the form so users can enter the date of joining the club.

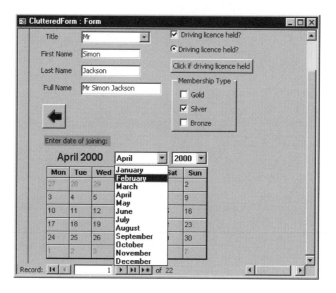

The control source for the calendar control has been set to a field in the `ClubMembers` table called `JoinDate` and this is where dates entered by users will be stored. If you set the Default Value for this field to be Date(), the calendar control will default to the current date.

As you can see, with its default settings the calendar control takes up a large area of 'form real estate'. This can be reduced considerably by tweaking its properties without reducing its ease of use.

This control has two sets of properties. It has the usual tabbed Property window but it also, if you double click on it (or try Edit, Calendar Object, Properties from the main menu), has a different set of properties, looking like this:

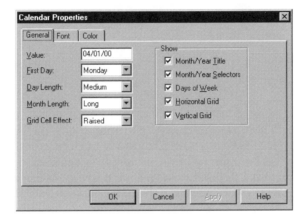

By reducing what the calendar shows (unchecking the Month/Year selectors, choosing the short Day Length display format, a flat Grid Cell Effect and so on) you can reduce considerably the space required.

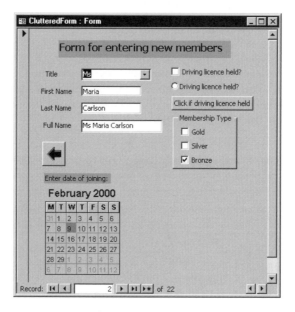

The choices you make depend on how your database is used. For instance, if new member records are added to the database shortly after their joining date, month and year selectors are largely unnecessary but if new records are only added every quarter, then a pop down list for moving between months becomes desirable. If you had a book database and were entering the publishing dates of tomes from Caxton onwards, then a pop down year selector would be vital too.

Further controls

The controls covered above should give you a reasonable collection for experimentation and you may find you never need anything further in the control line. You may, however, wish to skim through the rest of this chapter so you have an overview of what else is possible with Access controls but leaping to the next chapter is perfectly OK too.

Bound Object Frame

A bound object frame control displays a picture, a chart, a document or any object that can be stored in an OLE Object field. This control is bound to a field in an underlying table and that field must be of the OLE Object type. So, for example, you might use an OLE Object type in a contacts table to hold a picture of the person concerned. You could use a bound object frame control on a form to view the picture.

On the other hand, if the OLE object was an Excel worksheet, for instance, you could double click the control to open up Excel so the worksheet can be inspected. In other words, this control type permits the object to be edited (or even created) from within the form. This isn't always sensible, as with the photo example above, but you can choose whether to link to allow edits or not when you're entering records into the OLE Object field.

Open the `ClubMembers` table and you'll find a field called Photo and of type OLE Object. We provide three sample image files in the `AccSamp` folder which were created in Paint (`simon.bmp`, `maria.bmp` and `paula.bmp`). These should have been moved to your hard disk along with the sample Access files. The images can be used as portraits of the first three members in the table. To enter an object into the field, find the record relating to Simon Jackson, right mouse click on the OLE Object field and select Insert Object. Select the Create from File option and browse to the `simon.bmp` file, click the Link check box but not the Display as Icon check box.

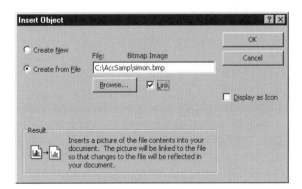

OK, so Simon's elegant image is now in the table and we want to see it in the form. You can achieve this automatically simply by getting Access to auto-generate a new form (try it to see) but we also want to show you how to do it manually. So, create a new form in Design view, drag a bound object frame control into place, delete the label (users are unlikely to need to be told that they're seeing members photos) and specify the control source of the frame itself as the OLE Object field. Save the form as `FurtherControls`.

If you also set the Size Mode (on the Format tab) to Stretch, each 'photo' neatly fills the available space; although there may be some distortion if you have made the dimensions of the control very different from those of the original image. If you double click on the image, you will find that you can give Simon a false moustache and/or red nose. If you feel that such power might be 'abused' by users of a real form that uses real photos (you know your users better than we do), you can disable editing with the Enabled setting on the Data tab: set it to No. Finally, I've copied the concatenated full name field from `ClutteredForm`, pasted it in under the bound frame and this is the result.

Unbound Object Frame

As described above, a bound object frame points to an object that is stored in the table. So Simon's picture appears on the form only when you are looking at his record. What if you want the same object (say a chart from an Excel worksheet) to appear on the form irrespective of which record is being displayed? OK, given the heading of this section, there are no prizes for guessing: you use an unbound object frame control. An unbound object frame control displays a picture, a chart etc. that is not stored in the underlying table and hence is not associated with any particular record. As with a bound object, it's possible to edit the file displayed with this type of control;

if it's displaying an .XLS file created with Excel, double clicking upon the image opens up Excel.

With this type of control, users could, for example, have access to a worksheet showing the current membership costs by double clicking an Excel icon on a form. As with the images, the values in this worksheet do not have to available for editing. Here I'll illustrate placing such a control on a form to give read-only access to membership rates.

Drag an unbound object control into place, select Create from File, browse to the file (charges.xls is in the same folder as the other sample files) and select the Display as Icon option but not the Link option.

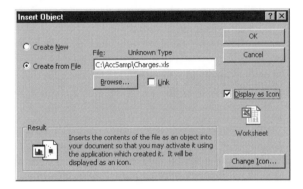

To change the icon or the label beneath, click the Change Icon button.

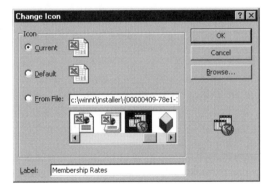

In the Properties list, set Enabled on the Data tab to Yes. This makes the control active in form view so that a double click on the icon launches Excel. The Locked property should be left set to Yes so that users can now inspect the worksheet by double clicking the icon on the form but will not be able to alter the data on the sheet.

Double clicking the worksheet icon opens Excel and displays the membership charges worksheet. (When Excel is open, the control is greyed out on the form).

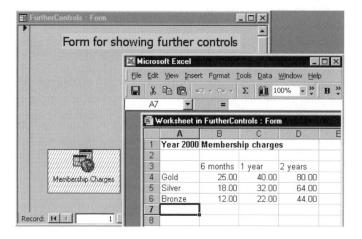

❡ *When I follow these steps to the point where Excel is on screen and I try to close it and return to the Access form, a 'software anomaly' appears. Excel remains visible and the Access title bar and the Access shortcut button in the bar that pops up from bottom of the screen start flashing. Clicking anywhere within Access closes Excel with a message telling you that any changes will not be saved.*

This seems only to occur the first time the unbound control is used: thereafter the Close button in Excel can be used to return smoothly to Access. No harm is done but it's a little messy. I suspect something isn't quite right here: maybe a point release or patch will clear up the confusion so you may not even see this effect. I only mention it in case it confuses you, as it did me on first sight.

Another oddity here is that, despite setting Locked to Yes, the Excel spreadsheet can, once it has performed its strange tricks the first time it's accessed, be edited by users. This is quite counter to what the help system and, indeed, common usage of the word 'locked', would suggest. Again, it is my hope that a service pack or point release of Access 2000 will cure this glitch. ❡

Summary

Despite all that this chapter has covered, it still isn't a full list of controls; we'll cover some more in Chapter 18. As we said earlier, controls are a very important part of Access!

In this chapter we've looked at putting sophisticated controls onto your forms. Choosing the right one for the job should be looked at both from the point of view of the data it lets into the table and from that of the user. The ease with which controls can be added, experimented with and removed lets you try several different approaches before deciding upon the one that's most suitable.

Chapter 12

Reports again – customizing printed output

Report types

Reports come in all shapes and sizes as we've already seen from a first play with the Report wizard in Chapter 6 and from the three types of AutoReport (the vanilla one from the New Object button and the Tabular and Columnar ones from the New button on the Database window).

It's worth taking another look at the Report wizard as it provides much flexibility in report construction; furthermore, a wizard-generated report is often the best starting point for a creating highly customized reports. A report is all about setting out information on the page and this is where the wizard really scores as it can produce a consistent layout very quickly. If it isn't exactly what you want, it's much easier to go to work on this approximation than to start from scratch. I almost invariably tinker with the wizard-generated report to fine tune it to my exact requirements.

Once again, it may not be immediately apparent what the wizard is going to do with some of the information it asks of you on the first run through. However, the reasons should become clear when you see the end result.

The Report wizard again

Open the `chap12start.mdb` file and go to the Reports tab. Click the New button to open the New Report window, choose a table (`ClubMembers`) and launch the Report wizard. Select some fields, as shown in the screenshot below

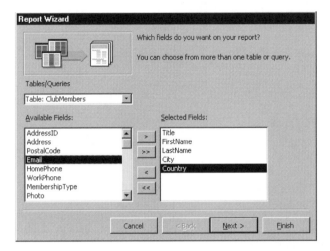

and click the Next button. Your choice in the second step determines the options the wizard will offer in a later step. If we set a grouping level here (something we didn't do in Chapter 6) you'll be able to choose from the six layout options shown in step four. So chose to group records by Country.

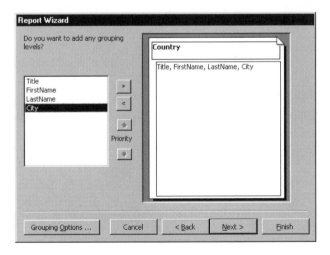

In the third step, elect to sort within the group by LastName.

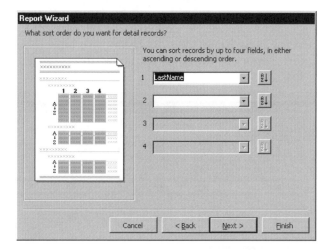

In the fourth step you can choose the layout of the report.

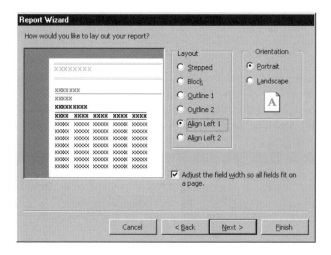

We looked at columnar and tabular AutoReports in Chapter 6 and if you thought such layouts were useful but that you could do with a bit more control over the fields, the sort order and so on, this will be a welcome sight. Pick one, say, Left Align 1, complete the wizard (our choices were Compact style and `CountryReport` as a title) and you should see something like this:

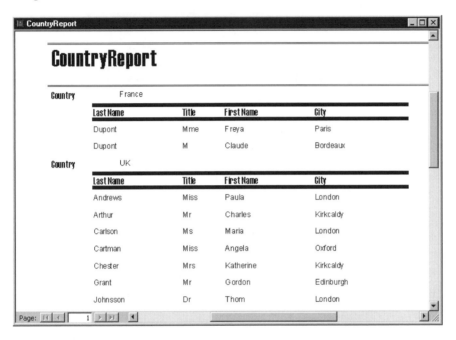

At this point the meaning of the groupings should became apparent. The report has found all of the records for club members in France and grouped them together. Within that group it has sorted them by last name.

Try running the wizard again but this time group the report by Country and City. This time there will be two levels of grouping in the report.

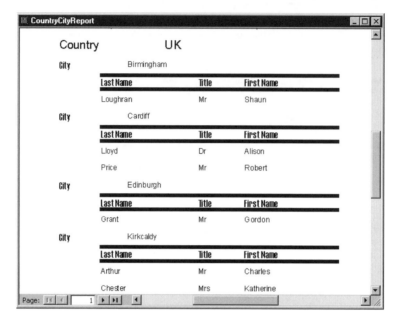

Now that you have an idea of what the wizard can do, run it again and try out the different layouts in step four to see what effects they produce.

The Label wizard

English is a wonderful language; it has words of astonishing subtlety. For example, I send out useful mail shots to my customers but I receive junk mail. It reminds me of the (probably apocryphal) sign seen in a shop:

> We buy junk,
> we sell antiques.

Whatever your views on mail shots (and, indeed, the long-term validity of snailmail), the ability to generate printed labels is still a major asset. Access handles the printing of labels as a specialized type of report and a label report can be based either on a table or on a query. We'll illustrate the latter option, so launch the wizard, select the EuropeMembers query and the first screen lets you choose your label size from dozens of sizes from several manufacturers.

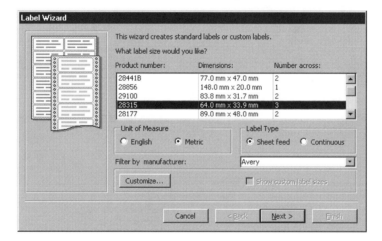

(In the unlikely event that none of these are suitable, you can click the Customize button to define a new label).

The next step lets you choose the font that will be printed on the label, its size, color and weight and whether it should be italicized or underlined.

In the third step you build a template for the printed labels, choosing the fields you want in the order you want them. Several fields can be placed on one line, which is very useful for concatenating first and last names. Double click on the `FirstName` field in the Available Fields list to move it into the Prototype Label, type a space and double click to add the last name field. Any characters you want to appear on every label can be added to the prototype too.

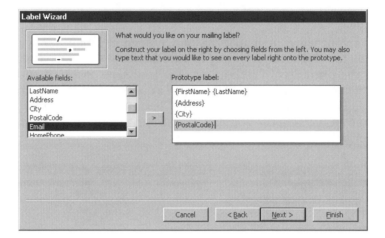

In the next step, labels can be sorted to print in a particular order, by city or by last name, or by city and then by last name. In the final step, name the new report as `MailingEurope` and click Finish to see a preview of the sheet of labels.

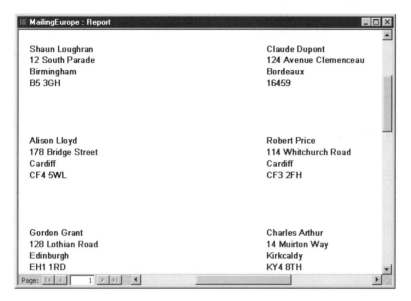

The Label wizard is a great time-saver (the longest part of the job is often finding a ruler so you can measure and identify the labels you are using) and once you've built a label report, you can use it time and time again.

The Chart wizard

Also in the New Report window is a Chart Wizard option. In Chapter 10, we covered the use of the chart wizard. Essentially this works just like the Chart wizard does when used in forms and charts, like labels, can be handled as reports.

Building a customized report

The time to investigate the tools offered in Design view is when a wizard-generated report doesn't look exactly right. You can, of course, design a report from scratch on a blank design screen but in is far more common to let the wizard do the grunt work and tweak the results.

Find or generate a report: here's mine, EmailList, in the Print Preview view.

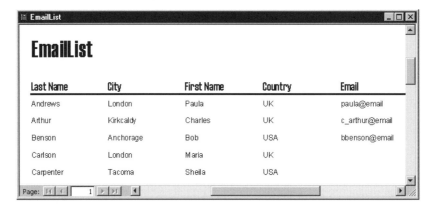

Now click the View button to see the Design view which should look familiar from the previous chapters on form design.

The design area itself looks somewhat different having rather more gray bands across it, labeled Detail, Page Header and Footer and Report Header and Footer. As you'd expect from exposure to forms in Design view, any objects in the Report Header are printed only once at the top of the first page and any Report Footer objects occur only at the very end of the report. Objects in the Page Header and Footer are printed at the top and bottom of each page. Objects in the Detail section are printed once for each record that is included in the report.

Text boxes and labels can be moved or removed in exactly the same way as they can on a form. Here you might decide that it's silly to have the city sandwiched between last and first names, so simply drag the labels and text boxes to new positions. Labels and text boxes in this report aren't linked in the same way as they are on forms so click on one and Shift-Click on the second to select a pair simultaneously, or by dragging a rubber band around/through them. Labels and text boxes can be moved together like this despite being in different sections of the report.

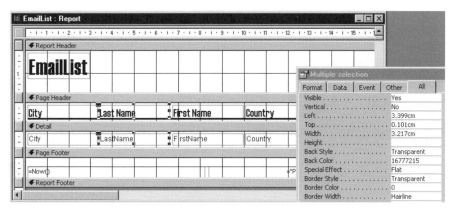

Flip between Design and Print Preview views as you work to see how things look.

The text in a label, such as the one in the header, can be edited by clicking twice to get a text-editing I-beam. These clicks should not be as close together as they are in a double click: double clicking highlights the whole entry which is fine if you want to, say, delete rather than edit it.

The reports illustrated above appear in the `chap12reports.mdb` file.

What else can you do on a report?

Sometimes you don't just want to print out the data from a table, you want to use it in some way. Access reports let you summarize data, calculate values and present fields in logical groups.

As a rule of thumb, most reports of any complexity are based upon a query. Queries are designed to make it easy to pull out specific information so the best approach is to design a query to locate all the records you need and add subtotals and totals during the report design stage.

To illustrate the further abilities of reports, I'll use the file `chap12start2.mdb` which is a tableful of specifications for widgets giving their shape, color, components and so on.

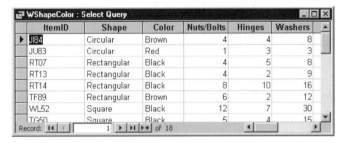

While this table won't bear scrutiny as a fine upstanding example of table crafting, it'll be fine for demonstration purposes.

Grouping data

As described above, the wizard lets you specify various levels of grouping. Using your skill and judgement, create a report that groups the widgets by shape and by color. My report, called `WidgetShapeColor`, is shown below.

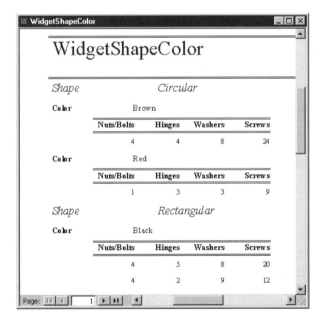

Looking at the Design view of this report

you can see the levels of grouping represented by the extra headers. There are the usual report and page headers but there's also a Shape Header and a Color Header. The labels and fields on the shape header appear every time a new shape is displayed in the report and those on the color header for each color within a group of shapes.

New groupings can be added to a wizard-generated report from the Design view by clicking on the Sorting and Grouping button in the main menu bar.

The present settings are displayed,

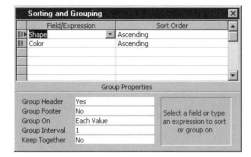

those which were chosen using the wizard. The Field/Expression column shows the fields on which records are sorted and/or grouped. The sort order is shown in the second column and the symbol to the left of the field name indicates that records are grouped by this field.

To sort the widgets by the number of nuts and bolts in the component, add the Nuts/Bolts field to the Field/Expression column, the Sort Order will default to Ascending and in the Group Properties panel, set the Group Header property to Yes. The grouping symbol appears alongside the Nuts/Bolts entry.

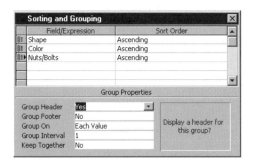

Close the dialog and the new Nuts/Bolts Header section is now in place. Into this section I want to place the Nuts/Bolts label and the associated text field. Drag the Nuts/Bolts label down from the Color Header section and the field up from the Detail section.

This is part of the result.

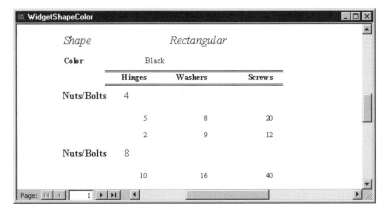

Hmmm. Not ideal, is it? I think the Hinges, Washers and Screws labels need to move down from the Color Header into the Nuts/Bolts Header section like this.

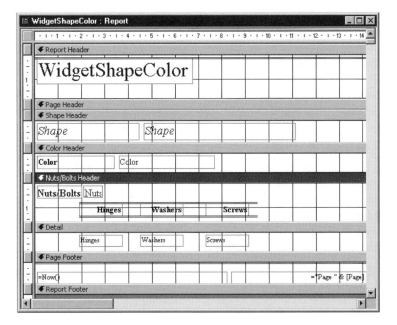

Thus, when seen in Design view, the report looks like this.

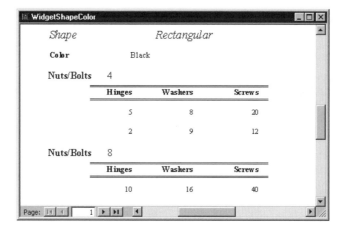

That's better.

By adding grouping levels, data can be displayed in a report that gives prominence to the information you wish to convey.

Summarizing data

This is where reports begin to add value to a report that's based on a simple table or query. In the example, we'll add subtotals for the number of widgets in each grouping for shape, color and nuts/bolts category and also a figure at the end of the report of the total value of all stock held.

To add the subtotal and total fields you build a field expression, that is to say an expression or formula that uses values from existing fields to calculate new data. As you've heard me say (or read me write) redundant data should not be stored in tables and therefore the Widget table doesn't store the value of stock held. However, from the values in the Price and Stock fields, the value of stocks held is easily calculated with a field expression.

Using field expressions

Make a copy of the WidgetShapeColor report, call it WidgetTotals. Place a new text box in the nuts/bolts header section. Give its label a memorable Name and set its Caption to read Stock Value. Call the text field itself something suitable, like StockCalc, and change its Format to Currency to match the data type of the Price field in the Widget table. For the Control

Source property, you can either type an expression straight into the cell or you can call up the Expression Builder. Create an expression that reads:

```
=Sum([Price]*[Stock])
```

which will multiply the value in the Price field by the value in the Stock field. Here it is as the Control Source property:

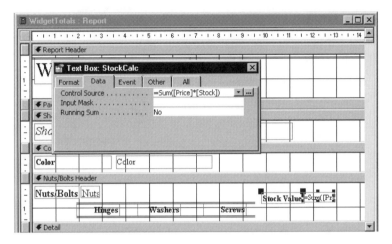

Flip to Report view and there's the calculated subtotal.

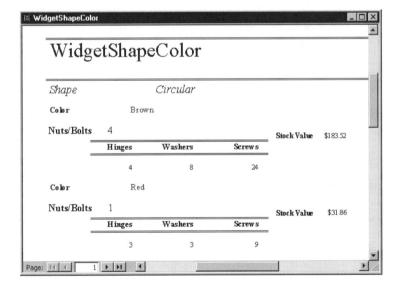

213

Back in Design view, copy the label and text field you've just created to the report footer, changing the label to read Total Stock Value. In Report view, you'll see that the total stock value has been calculated.

This is the last page of the report showing the two calculated fields generating two subtotals and the total stock value.

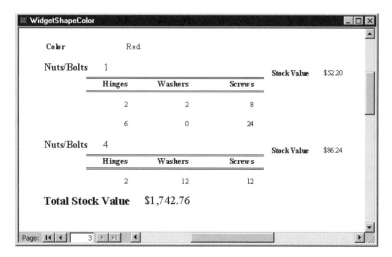

From this you can see that it is the position of a calculated field that determines how the calculation is performed: when placed in the nuts/bolts header section, it calculates the stock value of all the widgets that fall into each nuts/bolts category. When placed in the report footer, it calculates the stock value of all widgets in the report. If you were to place the same field expression in the color header section, it would calculate the stock value for all the widgets in each color category.

Both the reports based on the Widget table appear in the chap12end.mdb file.

Calculated fields can be very much more complex than this simple example. Access has a huge range of built-in functions for such tasks as handling dates (calculating the number of days between two dates, for example), for manipulating text and for calculating averages, standard deviations and the like. Very often, however, it's simple information like subtotals within categories and grand totals that make the difference between a clear and informative report and an impenetrable mass of data.

Formatting your report

The method of formatting the various elements of a report is exactly the same as that described for making formatting changes to a form, covered in Chapter 10.

Inspect the Properties list for the object to be formatted, locate the element you wish to change and edit its property accordingly. Constraint should be applied when designing reports too. The information you are trying to convey can become lost in too many fancy effects and irrelevant graphics so be abstemious with these additions.

Summary

An Access report is an immensely flexible method of preparing data for printing, adding value to the raw data by offering many ways of presenting it and illustrating it with charts. The same data can tell different stories depending on how a report is structured, so matching the report to the intended audience or to the point you are hoping to carry is worthwhile. This is often the hardest aspect of creating reports.

Chapter 13

Where are we now?

Single tables for simple databases

So far we have looked at databases where a single table holds all of the data in which we are interested at any one time. Queries, forms and reports have all been based either on that table or on queries that pull data from the one table. Using these components we have looked in detail at how Access makes it easy to extract, display and print out the data from a single table database.

The value of single table databases

A database that's straightforward and stores all its data in a single table can be the basis of a highly valuable application. There are many worthwhile types of single table databases, from address lists and Christmas card lists to inventories, small catalogs and many more. (If you are patiently waiting for the 'But', it's coming at the start of the next paragraph). If a single table solution is right for the task, despite its simplicity, then use just a single table. When I was a young database designer I built a database to collect medical information about patients. I almost bent over backwards to make it a multi-table application because I knew that this was what 'professional' database designers did. Luckily, common sense eventually prevailed and I built it with one table because that was all it needed.

Increasing complexity – most data isn't that simple

But, even though some applications do only need one table, life often isn't that simple. Databases almost invariably model some activity that's taking place in the real world with all its exceptions, variations and repetitions. Even the smallest of businesses run from the spare room or garage has customers, orders, price lists and suppliers of raw materials or components. A database to model something like that turns out to be much more efficient if each of the different object types (customers, suppliers etc.) is put into a separate table; i.e. all of the customers in one table, all of the suppliers in another and so on.

The whys and wherefores that make this so are covered in Part IV. Hopefully, in Parts I to III we have given you a firm grounding in how to use the basic components of Access – tables, queries, forms and reports. If you've worked through that, you are now in an excellent position to understand both why we need to use multiple tables and how to use them effectively.

So let's get started.

Part IV

More complex databases

Chapter 14

Multiple table databases

More is better!

The natural progression from a single table database is to a multiple table database. At its most basic, this means that instead of one base table containing all the data, the data is split between a number of base tables. How many tables you need depends on what you are doing: a database for a small business might have three or four tables, Northwind, the sample database that Microsoft supplies with Access, contains eight while a big financial application is likely to have hundreds.

Using multiple tables to store your data

Using multiple tables to store your data has several advantages. These are best illustrated, not by us telling you to do it, but by showing you the problems that arise when a single table is used to hold data that's more complex than it has been in our previous examples. The idea behind this approach is simple – motivation.

Using multiple tables is obviously more complex than using a single one and you are going to have to put effort into finding out how the multiple tables can be induced to work together. However, if we can convince you that the gain far outweighs the initial pain (and it does) then we hope that you'll embrace the idea of multiple tables with open arms.

So, a brief motivational diversion.

Imagine a microbrewery selling several different beers by the bottle. The database needs to store each order and the fields required might be these:

OrderID	OrderDate	Item	Quantity	Price	and several more for the customer's name and address

You may also want to store the name of the staff member who made the sale. And since there is only one table in the database, you'll have to include any other information that you want to store about that person (such as date of birth, date of employment and home address) in the same table. So we need to add these fields:

EmployeeID	LastName	FirstName	DateOfBirth	DateOfEmployment	and more for the employee's address

Each record in the resulting table might look like this, though we're not showing all the fields as there's not enough room on the page.

OrderID	Customer	Item	Quantity	Price	EmpID	LastName	FirstName	DOB
1	Carr	Druid's Dream	6	$4.65	7	Johnston	Hannah	03/05/72
2	Jones	Adder Ale	1	$5.50	8	Murray	Bert	12/10/48
3	Smith	Adder Ale	2	$5.50	7	Johnston	Hannah	03/05/72
4	Jones	Lambswool	1	$5.50	2	Trudeau	Simone	23/08/58
5	Carr	Adder Ale	2	$5.50	2	Trudeau	Simone	23/08/58
6	Thomas	Druid's Dream	12	$4.65	7	Johnston	Hannah	03/05/72
7	Forbes	Druid's Dream	6	$4.65	8	Murray	Bert	12/10/48
8	Smith	Adder Ale	4	$5.50	8	Murray	Bert	12/10/48

Problem 1: redundant data

In the table above, there are many occasions where the same information appears in many records; the addresses of the sales people, for example. This repeated data is also known as 'redundant data'.

So what's wrong with a bit of redundant data? Well, as the table grows (with increasing orders) the burden of redundant data can become huge. It takes up space, it makes the table large and unwieldy and has the effect of making queries run slowly. And you will get very bored entering the same data over and over and over again.

Problem 2: typographical errors
Human beings are only human and entering data can be a rather boring task, especially if each order is often largely a repeat of the previous one. The opportunities for error are many: before long, records will appear in which Hannah's name is spelled Hanna, where Bert was born in 1918 and Druid's Dram is offered for sale (an appropriate enough name but incorrect nevertheless).

These errors start to do serious damage when queries are used to extract information. Hannah is unlikely to be pleased if she's paid on commission and isn't credited with sales accredited to Hanna. Someone might decide to retire the octogenarian on the staff and the business plan might be put in jeopardy because sales of Druid's Dream aren't going as well as usual.

Problem 3: updating records
Simone gets married and decides that she will change her last name to that of her husband. It's a lot of work to find all the records of her sales and edit each one.

Problem 4: modifying records
If the record for order number four is deleted, all reference to the Lambswool brew is lost because its name and price are stored nowhere else in the table. Furthermore, a new brew called Hector's Nectar comes on line. There's nowhere for its name and price to be stored, so you must wait until an order is taken before it can be entered and if you wanted to generate a price list of all brews to include the new variety, you couldn't.

These are some of the problems that arise in single table databases when the complexity of the data increases. In fact, there are more, and poor long-suffering students on database courses get a much longer list. The good news is that all are addressed by designing a multi-table database. True, you can probably think of alternative individual cures – the last name change could be implemented with an update query, for instance, and an incomplete dummy record could inhabit the table until the first order for the new brew is taken. However, experience has shown that a multi-table solution is the most comprehensive treatment for all these woes.

OK, enough motivation, how do we do it?

Deciding what data goes into which table

As was said in the last chapter, a database frequently models an activity that's taking place in the 'real' world. In these activities, objects can usually be identified readily. These aren't objects in any special mathematical sense, just elements that can be combined to define the activity.

In the microbrewery example above, a customer is an object, as are a member of staff, a brew and an order. It is also clear that objects fall into groups that are likely to have similar information stored about them. For example, one customer is one object, another customer is a different object and an order is a third object. However, the type of information that we want to store about the customers differs from the information that we want to store about the order. We can group similar objects into object types and it is a good rule of thumb that the information about each object type should be stored in a separate table. So here we might have four tables called `Customer`, `Staff`, `Product` and `Order`.

To illustrate the mechanics of dividing a single table of data into multiple tables of data, we'll start from a slightly simpler version of the microbrewery table shown above. The table, called `BrewSales`, is in the `chap14start.mdb` file and looks like this:

OrderID	Customer	Item	Quantity	Price
1	Carr	Druid's Dream	6	$4.65
2	Jones	Adder Ale	1	$5.50
3	Smith	Adder Ale	2	$5.50
4	Jones	Lambswool	1	$5.50
5	Carr	Adder Ale	2	$5.50
6	Thomas	Druid's Dream	12	$4.65
7	Forbes	Druid's Dream	6	$4.65
8	Smith	Adder Ale	4	$5.50

❛ *This is, as you'll have noticed, a very small table because we've removed most of the detail and the reference to employees. It is, however, large enough to illustrate the concepts behind dividing data between tables.* ❜

First we decide to split out the customer information and put it in a Customer table, adding an ID field of the AutoNumber type to ensure that each entry is unique.

CUSTOMER

CustomerID	Customer
1	Carr
2	Jones
3	Smith
4	Thomas
5	Forbes

In a real example, you're likely to have additional fields for address, contact details and so on.

Then we decide to split out all the product information and put it into a Product table, again adding an AutoNumber ID field.

PRODUCT

ProductID	Item	Price
1	Adder Ale	$5.50
2	Druid's Dream	$4.65
3	Lambswool	$5.50

This leaves us with a mere two fields, OrderID and Quantity, for the Order table. On their own, these two don't tell us what was bought or who bought it, so two fields must be added to access that information in the newly formed Customer and Product tables. These are CustomerID and ProductID.

ORDER

OrderID	Quantity	CustomerID	ProductID
1	6	1	2
2	1	2	1
3	2	3	1
4	1	2	3
5	2	1	1
6	12	4	2
7	6	5	2
8	4	3	1

The first record in this table tells us that customer 1 bought six of product 2; looking back at the Customer and Product tables reveals that customer 1 is Carr and that product 2 is Druid's Dream.

OK, so now customer and product details are only stored once each, which is good, but we're left to deal with an unfriendly number-filled `Order` table, which is bad. Fear not, when the completed database is in use you'll rarely, if ever, see the table looking like this. Using queries and forms, Access can present the data in a helpful format so you can see at a glance

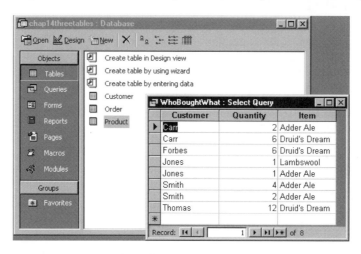

that customer Jones has bought Lambswool and Adder Ale and that Thomas has only tried Druid's Dream. The `WhoBoughtWhat` query above shows who bought which products, a typical example of the appearance your data would have in use.

In the `chap14manualsplit.mdb`, you'll find the data from the original `BrewSales` table split into three tables (`Customer`, `Product` and `Order`) as described above and the `WhoBoughtWhat` query.

The subsequent chapters will look at designing a multi-table database from scratch, but what can you do if you realize that the data in your current table would benefit from being split into several tables? Do you really have to begin all over again? Happily not. Access comes with a Table Analyzer wizard that automates the process of splitting a single table into as many tables as it deems necessary. It makes a reasonably good stab at the job too. It's a worthwhile route to try (with a backup of your database, of course) as it doesn't take long and you can make tweaks when following the wizard's steps, as shown below. If you don't like the result, you can always go for a manual redesign.

Start by opening the `chap14start2.mdb` file, containing the familiar `BrewSales` table.

Build a quick AutoForm based on the `BrewSales` table and call it `BrewSalesForm` – this will be used later but, once built, can be forgotten for the moment.

Using the Table Analyzer wizard

To run the Table Analyzer wizard, find the Analyze button in the main button bar. It will probably be showing this icon.

If it is, click it, but if it isn't, click the slim button with an arrowhead to its right and pick Analyze Table.

The first two steps describe, as in the paragraphs above, the potential problems with single table solutions and the potential benefits of using multiple tables. You don't have to do anything except read, looking at the examples if you wish, and click Next to proceed. In the third step, select the table you require analyzed.

❛ *Also on the third screen you can decide whether you want to see the introductory screens next time you run the Analyzer.* ❜

Here we're using `BrewSales` so highlight it and click Next. Now you decide whether to give the wizard its head or whether to divide the table yourself. The wizard's decision is not final, so let's see what it produces by accepting the default 'Yes, let the wizard decide'. Click Next.

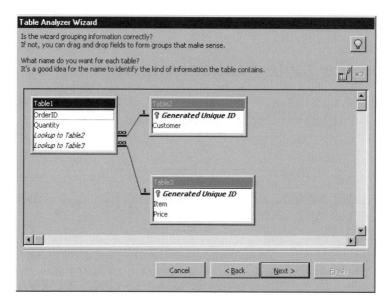

The wizard has divided the table into three. Table2 contains the customer records and Table3 contains the product details. Both tables have acquired a Generated Unique ID field. Table1 retains the order details and has gained some new Lookup fields: these are what will enable Access to locate all the elements of a single order now that the fields are located in different tables.

It's worth noting that you need a certain amount of data to enable to wizard to function properly. If the `BrewSales` table is shrunk to just the first seven records, the wizard decides that it doesn't have enough sample data upon which to work.

It is apparent that the wizard agrees with our theoretical identification of objects performed above and our answer to the question at the top of the page ('Is the wizard grouping information correctly?') is therefore yes, so we'll proceed to the second question. With the focus on Table1, click the rename button to the right of the question, type `Order` in the box and click OK. Repeat this for the other two tables, choosing names to reflect the table contents, like `Customer` and `Product`.

Click Next to continue: this step asks you to confirm the wizard's identification of primary key fields. These are the Generated Unique ID fields it added to the `Customer` and `Product` tables. The `Order` table doesn't have a primary key, however, so highlight the `OrderID` field and click this button.

If there wasn't an obvious candidate for a primary key field, one can be generated (as was done automatically for the other two tables) by clicking this button.

The three tables now all have meaningful names and primary keys.

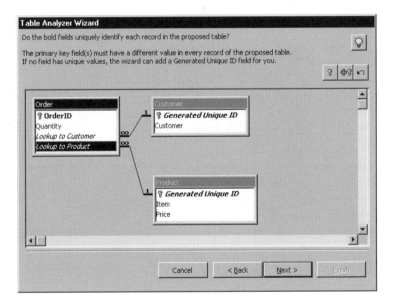

Click Next. The default in the last page is for the wizard to create a query to display your records just as they were in the original single table: this is a useful starting point so select the 'Yes, create the query' option. If the check box at the bottom of this step remains selected, Help will open automatically when the query is displayed. For simplicity's sake, I've unchecked it. Click Finish

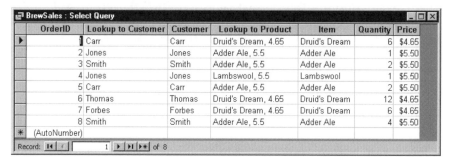

	OrderID	Lookup to Customer	Customer	Lookup to Product	Item	Quantity	Price
▶	1	Carr	Carr	Druid's Dream, 4.65	Druid's Dream	6	$4.65
	2	Jones	Jones	Adder Ale, 5.5	Adder Ale	1	$5.50
	3	Smith	Smith	Adder Ale, 5.5	Adder Ale	2	$5.50
	4	Jones	Jones	Lambswool, 5.5	Lambswool	1	$5.50
	5	Carr	Carr	Adder Ale, 5.5	Adder Ale	2	$5.50
	6	Thomas	Thomas	Druid's Dream, 4.65	Druid's Dream	12	$4.65
	7	Forbes	Forbes	Druid's Dream, 4.65	Druid's Dream	6	$4.65
	8	Smith	Smith	Adder Ale, 5.5	Adder Ale	4	$5.50
*	(AutoNumber)						

Record: 1 of 8

and this is the resulting answer table, called BrewSales. Well, it doesn't look quite like the original; indeed there's a lot more going on in here. You can see that Access is able to pull together records from different tables to build a full record showing all that the original table held, with some extra Lookup fields. It may not be instantly apparent what good these fields are doing: they just seem to be repeating data shown in other fields.

Take a quick look at what's in the Tables tab – this isn't avoiding the issue, it's a digression that will, hopefully, make things clearer in a moment.

The three new tables are there (`Order`, `Product` and `Customer`) plus the original table upon which the Analyzer was run, renamed as `BrewSales_OLD`. In the Forms tab is the `BrewSalesForm` which was based on the original `BrewSales` table. Now that there's no table called `BrewSales` (because it's been renamed), can we expect the form to work properly? Try it and see.

Wonder of wonders, there it is looking perfect. How does Access work this magic?

When you created that form it was based on the table called `BrewSales`, so when you opened the form, it looked for a table called `BrewSales` and pulled the data from there. Or, to be slightly more accurate, it didn't look for a table called `BrewSales`, it looked for a table or query called `BrewSales`. Then the Analyzer renamed the table and created a query with the original name. So now when you fire up the form, it finds a query with the expected name and is quite happy to pull data from that.

❢ *One consequence of the fact that a form can pull data from a table and/or a query is that, just as Access won't let you create two tables with the same name, you can't have a table and a query with identical names.* ❞

You can create a new AutoForm based on this query which should look like this one, called `BrewSalesForm2`.

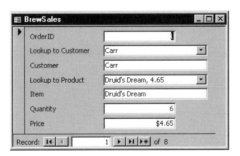

If you click on the arrowhead in the Lookup to Customer and Lookup to Product fields, you'll see ready-made combo boxes from which you can make selections. These are ideal on a form for entering new records. A quick flip into Design view to delete the Customer, Item and Price fields that show details that are duplicated by the lookup fields leaves you with a lean, mean data-entry form.

The file chap14wizardsplit.mdb contains the tables, query and forms described above.

To illustrate the next two points, open the chap14start3.mdb file, which contains tables called MoreComplex and BrewSalesTypo.

What if...

What if you don't like the division of data that the wizard proposes? In the example shown below, in which the Analyzer wizard has been let loose on the table called `MoreComplex`,

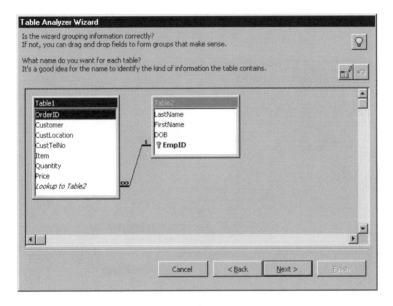

the suggested configuration would still lead to multiple instances of customer details in Table1.

To subdivide Table1 by relocating the customer records in a third table, click on the `Customer` field and drag it to some free space: the cursor shows as a tiny table. Release the mouse button and Table3 appears containing the `Customer` field and a Generated Unique ID field. This new field will ensure that each customer has an unique ID number for accurate identification. Rename Table3 in the dialog box that pops up. Now the `CustLocation` and `CustTelNo` fields can be dragged across into the new table.

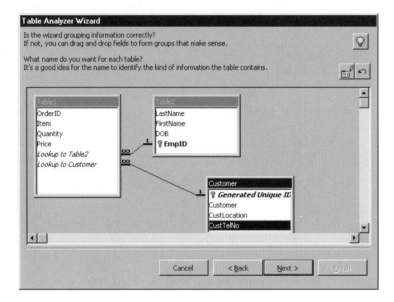

Once you're happy with your alterations (in this example, you might also consider a fourth table for product details) rename the other tables as necessary and continue as outlined above.

And what if?

What if the Analyzer wizard pops an extra step, not covered above, that looks like this? Run the wizard against the `BrewSalesTypo` table, proceed as before and you'll see this step:

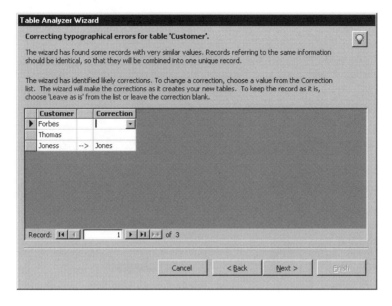

Here the wizard attempts to identify records with entries so similar that they might be typos and it also tries to identify sensible corrections.

In the `Customer` column in this example there are three names. The first two are correct (Forbes and Thomas) so pop down the list as select (Leave as is) in the `Correction` column for them both.

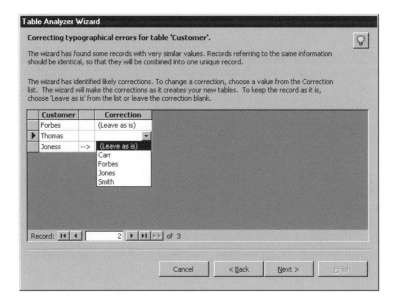

The third entry, Joness, has been correctly identified as a mis-spelling of Jones, with the correct spelling shown in the `Correction` column.

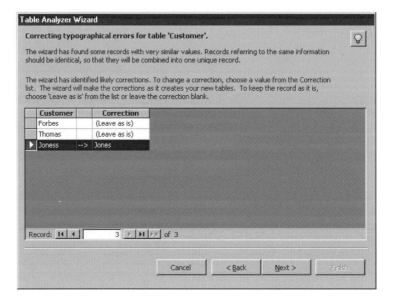

If the `Correction` column didn't contain the correct spelling, you'd click to pop down the list of possible corrections and select one, or tell the wizard to leave it as it is.

If the wizard doesn't spot any such typos, you won't see this step.

As the `MoreComplex` and `BrewSalesTypo` tables are just examples of tweaking the Analyzer's division of your data, we don't, for once, have an `chap14end.mdb`.

Summary

The bigger the database, the more important it is to design it with a multi-table structure. Databases have a habit of growing and becoming more complex. Often what happens is that users find a database application easy to use and want it to do more and to store details of other aspects of the business. As the complexity increases, it becomes more likely that you'll encounter the four problems outlined above. The time and effort spent in redesigning the contents of a single table into a series of tables will almost invariably be less than that taken to work around the problems.

If the Table Analyzer doesn't produce the results you hope for, designing from scratch is the next step. Creating a database from the ground up also gives you a much greater insight into the way a multi-table database works.

Once you've identified the various objects about which data is stored and constructed tables to contain those objects, the next stage is to determine how the tables should act together to form the whole database. No prize is offered for guessing that this happens in Chapter 15.

Tables – making multiple tables work together

In Chapter 14 we tried to convince you that it was a good idea to split data up into separate tables in the database. However, in order for a database that's constructed from multiple tables to work effectively, there has to be some means of 'associating' the data from the different tables so that, although it is located in different tables, it can work together. In Access, and indeed in RDBMSs in general, the associations between tables are called 'joins'.

The data in the tables needs to be regulated somewhat more carefully in a multi-table database and Access uses primary keys to do this. Primary keys ensure that each record can be identified uniquely and this property is important in defining the joins that are made between tables.

The primary keys and joins work together to enable Access to identify the records from different tables that comprise a complete set of data.

OK, that was a brief outline of how a multi-table Access database is put together, but it doesn't tell you how all of this works. So, here comes the detail.

Primary keys

Primary keys are, as we've said, a way of ensuring that each of the records stored in a database can be identified uniquely. Even if Mr Smith does order five red roses twice on the 14th of February (let's not ask why), the database should record two different events and ensure that we don't confuse them. Even if all of the other fields in the `Order` table carry the same value, the primary key value (in this case found in the `OrderNo` field) enables us to differentiate between the two events.

OrderNo	Name	Date	Type	Number
32	Smith	14th Feb	Red Roses	5
33	Jones	14th Feb	White Roses	6
34	Simons	14th Feb	Red Roses	6
35	Smith	14th Feb	Red Roses	5

This table is relatively simple but primary keys assume even more importance in a multi-table database.

Deciding on a primary key field

Every table should have a primary key. Access can automatically add a field if you use the wizard to create a table, the additional field being of AutoNumber type. As we have covered earlier, the values in AutoNumber fields are automatically filled in for you with the values 1, 2, 3 and so on. This, of course, ensures a unique value in each record. In Design view, you define the primary key field yourself. So which field should you pick?

Primary keys ensure uniqueness so your choice should be a field that is unlikely to contain duplicate entries. You'll often find that something is already used to identify objects uniquely, for instance, a National Insurance or Social Security number. This makes an ideal primary key field in a personnel table. Products are identified by a code or serial number, cars have unique license plates (or are supposed to!) and so on.

If there isn't an obvious candidate, you can add an AutoNumber field to generate a unique ID number for each record.

Adding a primary key

When you've decided on all the fields in a table and have identified the field to contain the primary key, the actual act of declaring the primary key field is extremely simple. Click on the field name and then on the Primary Key button.

A tiny key symbol appears to the left of the field name, signifying that this is now a primary key field.

It is common practice for the primary key field to be the first field in a table. This is by no means obligatory, but our feeling is that it is a convention worth following. To insert a field at the top of the list, click on the current top field, on Insert from the main menu, select Rows and a new row is inserted.

You can remove the primary key field designation equally easily, by selecting the field and clicking the Primary Key button again. Decisions about primary keys are best made at the design stage before any data is entered into the table. You can change things later but it's not quite as easy.

Joins – and foreign keys

A join is created between two tables starting with a primary key field in one of the tables. The field in the second table at the 'other end' of the join is called a foreign key field. Which bring us to an interesting point. As the database designer you explicitly tell Access which fields are the primary key fields. But foreign keys only come into existence when joins are created between tables. In a sense, the act of creating a join is the one that tells Access which field is the foreign key. I don't want all of this to sound too existentialist, I only mention it because otherwise you may think you have missed a stage somewhere when we run through this in practice.

In a single table database (where it's still highly sensible to have a primary key field to ensure the uniqueness of records) there will be no foreign key fields. But that changes as soon as you start to use multiple tables.

Identifying a foreign key field

To illustrate this, we'll return to the three tables that were identified from the original single microbrewery table. They look like this (with rather minimal data, just to save paper):

PRODUCT

⚷ ProductID	Item	Price
1	Adder Ale	5.50
2	Druid's Dream	4.65
3	Lambswool	5.50

CUSTOMER

⚷ CustomerID	Customer
1	Carr
2	Jones
3	Smith

ORDER

⚷ OrderID	CustomerID	ProductID	Quantity
1	1	2	6
2	2	1	1
3	3	1	2

❛ *The key symbol shown above identifies the primary key fields. These are just shown in this book, they don't appear like this in Access.* ❜

The Order table tells you that customer 1 bought product 2. It is intuitively obvious (he typed hopefully) that, using the other two tables, we can see that customer 1 is Carr and that product 2 is Druid's Dream.

So the CustomerID field in the Customer table should be joined to the field of the same name in the Order table and the ProductID field in the Product table should be joined to the ProductID field in the Order table.

The CustomerID field in the Customer table is a primary key field but in the Order table the CustomerID field is going to be the foreign key field, as is the ProductID field in the Order table: you have now identified the two fields that will be used as foreign key fields.

Armed with this knowledge, you're in a position to make the joins.

Joining tables

Joins must be made between fields of the same data type. A text string in one table and a currency value in another doesn't sound like a match made in heaven: Access certainly doesn't think so because it won't allow you to form a join between two fields unless they are of the same data type.

The only exception to this rule is when (as often happens) you use an AutoNumber field as a primary key. In this case, the other end of the join (the foreign key field) must be of the Number: Long Integer type. This, too, makes sense on further inspection. When you use the AutoNumber type, you hand over to Access the generation of a unique number for each record so it automatically puts a number into the field. However, the numbers that Access inserts are, in reality, simply long integer numbers so that's the data type to use for the foreign key.

Making joins between tables

To illustrate the joining process we'll use the microbrewery `Order`, `Product` and `Customer` tables that have become familiar, contained in the file `chap15start.mdb`. This is still a very simple database with limitations for use in the real world, the most restrictive of which is that a customer may only order a single product per order, but it will suffice for demonstration purposes.

Click on the Relationships button in the main button bar:

This opens the relationship window, a blank gray window, on top of which is the Show Table window.

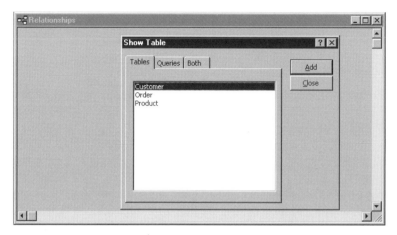

If you don't see the Show Table window, click the Show Table button.

From the Tables tab, double click on each of the tables in the relationship to place them in the relationship window (or highlight them and click Add). We're using `Customer`, `Order` and `Product`. Now close the Show Table window.

The three tables are now in place and you're ready to make the first join. As discussed above, the `CustomerID` field in the `Customer` table is to be joined to the `CustomerID` field in the `Order` table. Click on the `CustomerID` field in the `Customer` table and (holding the mouse button down) drag it across to the `Order` table: when the cursor reaches the `Order` table, it shows as a tiny field. Release the mouse button when the cursor is over the `CustomerID` field. A dialog box pops out, entitled Edit Relationships.

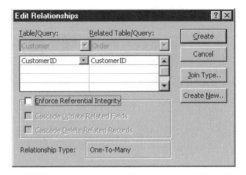

Reading down from the top of the box, Access identifies the fields and tables with which you're working. Then comes a check box labeled Enforce Referential Integrity with two further check boxes grayed out. This sounds rather like a draconian edict issued by Big Brother but is, in fact, Access asking whether it should work behind the scenes to ensure that duff data doesn't sneak into your database. It's a Good Thing and you should check the box.

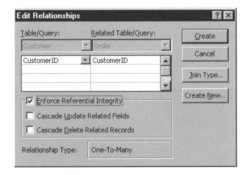

More questions arise as the grayed out boxes spring to life. Are Cascade Update Related Fields and Cascade Delete Related Records also Good Things? Yes, they can be amazingly useful, depending upon circumstances. However, when you're learning and experimenting it's probably best to leave these two unchecked for the moment. As your confidence in using Access and controlling your data grows, you can return and enable either one or both of them. But of course, by writing that we have undoubtedly made you almost insanely keen to know what they do. So...

❛ *Cascade Update and Cascade Delete*

These settings allow Access to automate the housekeeping tasks of updating or deleting records that, in a multi-table database, are spread between many tables. For example, suppose you set Cascade Delete on the join between a `Customer` *table and an* `Order` *table. If you then ever delete a customer's record from the* `Customer` *table, Access would automatically delete the records of every purchase that customer ever made. In general, this move won't please your accountant, so Cascade Delete is inappropriate in this case. On the other hand, there are cases where Cascade Delete is appropriate; in a database that's storing information about potential orders, for example.*

Cascade Update enables you to change the primary key value for a customer even when that customer has placed orders. Both of these options are reasonable powerful and need to be treated with respect since they can wreak havoc when used incautiously. The flip side of that is that they are really useful when used properly so regard them as friends. ❜

At the bottom of the dialog it says Relationship Type: One-To-Many. Types of relationship, of which one-to-many is one, are covered below. For the time being, just accept the default and click the Create button.

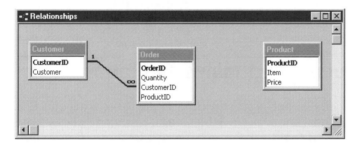

In the relationships window you should see a line running between the two fields to indicate the join is in place. There's a tiny one alongside the `Customer` table end of the line and a tiny infinity symbol (a figure of eight on its side) at the `Order` end. These indicate the one (1) and many (∞) ends of the join. This is reasonable since one customer can, and hopefully will, place many orders.

Repeat this process to place a join between the `ProductID` field in the `Product` table and the `ProductID` field in the `Order` table. Set the referential integrity as before and the relationships window should show these joins.

❦ *At this point it might be worthwhile dragging the tables around until they sit with the `Order` table in the middle and the joins show without the complication of crossing lines. When you're working with several tables it's very helpful to be able to spread them out in a pattern that displays the joins clearly. The layout is saved when you close the relationship window.* ❧

That's it. It has taken us some time to describe this all, but in practice the process is very easy to use and only takes a few seconds to set up.

How joins affect tables and forms

We'll now take a brief look at the three tables to see what effect introducing joins has had. The `Order` table looks just as it always did but the `Customer` and `Product` tables have acquired an extra expand button to the left of each record. The `Customer` table looks like this:

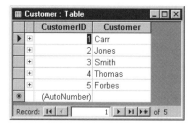

When you click the expand button by the first record, a subtable pops out showing the associated records from the Order table.

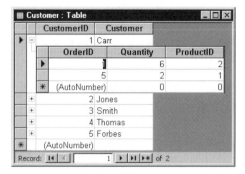

Access has automatically given tables at the 'one' end of a join expand buttons to let you see records in the table at the 'many' end of the join.

If you build an AutoForm on the Customer table, this too will automatically include a subform to view the data in the Order table.

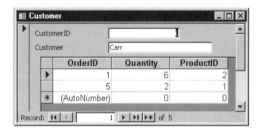

Indexing

We said in Chapter 8 that fields can be indexed and that foreign key fields were almost always worth indexing. We say it again here, even more forcefully: it is a very good idea to index all foreign key fields in your database. The reason is that when you run a query that uses data from more than one table, Access will have to search through the data in one or more of the foreign keys. If those fields are indexed, the answer to the query will appear more rapidly. If you have large tables of data, this can make a difference of an order of magnitude or more.

Join types

As a break from the practical work, we'll use the rest of this chapter to describe the different types of join that you can set up. If you are really keen to keep on working, you may want to skip this for now and come back to it later. On the other hand, we put it here because it seemed the most logical place for it, so if you can bear it...

One-To-Many relationships

This is by far the most common type of relationship between tables (the other two are One-To-One and Many-To-Many).

❛ *One-To-Many and its friends are also known as joins; in fact both terms are reasonably commonly used.* ❜

A one-to-many relationship indicates that one record from one table may be joined to one or more records in the second table. In our example, you'd hope that your customers would place many orders and buy from you again and again. Each purchase means a record in the `Order` table that's joined to a single customer record in the `Customer` table. It's the same with orders for products: each brew is likely to be ordered many times. The relationship between the `Product` table and the `Order` table is also a one-to-many join.

❛ *Given the business we're discussing, perhaps we should call it a one-too-many join...* ❜

One-To-One relationships

These are rare but can be useful. This type of join ensures that a single record on one table is always and only joined to a single record in the second table.

An example of its use would be if you had a table of contact details and that one or two of those contacts went abroad for extended periods. You decide not to store these temporary addresses in the contacts table because most people in the table don't have a foreign address, so you put them in a separate table. With a one-to-one join between this table and the contacts table, each foreign address would be associated only and always to one contact.

Many-To-Many relationships

Describing joins as many-to-many is almost a misnomer as they are constructed with two one-to-many joins used in a specific way. A many-to-many join means that many records from one table can be joined to many records in the second table by making use of a third table as an intermediary.

In our example, a customer can buy many different products and each product can be bought by many different customers. A many-to-many join between the `Customer` and `Product` table can therefore be envisaged with the `Order` table acting as the intermediate table. In the practical session above, we made two one-to-many joins (one between `Customer` and `Order` and one between `Product` and `Order`). This, in effect, defines a many-to-many join between the `Customer` and `Product` tables, using `Order` as the intermediate table.

Not all pairs of one-to-many joins form a many-to-many join, however. (It couldn't be that simple, could it?) The two one-to-many joins must have their 'many' ends in the same table, as does the relationship you've just built. Two one-to-many joins like this

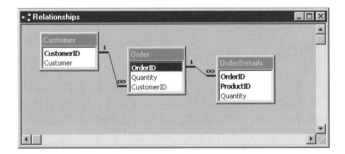

do not constitute a many-to-many join. They're just two one-to-many joins between `Customer` and `Order` (one customer can place many orders) and `OrderDetails` and `Order` (one order can be for many items).

❢ *The additional table would mean that a customer could order more than one product at a time. The* Product *table is still required and would be joined to* OrderDetails *like this. This does produce a many-to-many join which is between the* Order *and* Product *tables.*

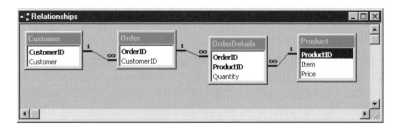

❦

Incidentally, the OrderDetails table is an example of one in which it is useful to use a primary key composed of two fields – in this case OrderID and ProductID. This is because, in any one order, we would only expect any one product to appear once. True, the person placing the order may want six of that product, but that is recorded in the Quantity field.

In the chap15twofieldPK.mdb file you'll find four tables related in this way with a primary key composed of two fields.

Editing joins

If your cursor slips and you inadvertently join the wrong fields or if you forget to set referential integrity (in which case the 1 and ∞ symbols would not be shown alongside the join line) it's easy to edit the join.

Double click on a join line to bring up the Edit Relationship dialog to change the fields or the referential integrity settings.

Deleting joins

Click on the join you want to delete (it becomes fatter when you've selected it) and press the Delete key. Access checks that you're sure; when you answer Yes, the join is removed.

Summary

In Chapter 14 we discussed the reasons why a multi-table database can be a better tool than a single table database and illustrated how a table can be subdivided. In this chapter you've learned how to join the new tables so that they can be used together by Access to provide the same level of functionality as the old single table. The joins are in place for inspection in the microbrewery database in the `chap15end.mdb` file.

Next we'll construct a complete example to bring together these elements into a working database.

Chapter 16

Tables – a complete multi-table database

Data – divide and conquer

When you begin work on any new database project, it is best to start with pencil, paper and a cup of coffee well away from the computer. This isn't simply to keep the coffee out of the keyboard, the real reason is because the process is one that requires thought in a peaceful environment. In the light of what you wish to extract from the finished database, consider what you need to store in it. In fact, that last sentence contains an important point which is often overlooked. When people start to design a database, they often ask the question 'What data do I want to store?'. A much better question to ask is 'What information do I ultimately want to extract from the database?'. Once you have answered that one, you will be in a much better position to decide what information you should store. It is also useful, as discussed in Chapter 14, to identify the various objects that will form the basis of the tables and then to think about how the objects are related.

In our next example, the data to be divided and conquered is for a catalog of books. Four 'objects' (see end of chapter) have been identified – the books themselves, their category (fiction, humor, poetry etc.) the authors and the publishing houses. Starting from scratch we'll create a complete set of tables and joins in this chapter and the following chapters will build on this database. Using the other three elements of a database – queries, forms and reports – will be covered with reference to multiple tables.

Although our example database will again be compact, one of the joys of a multi-table database is that it is very flexible. If you start selling books, you can add a customer table and an order table, and to track which sales assistants are selling which books, all you need add is a table of staff.

This example, however, will restrict itself to just four tables.

Building the tables

The definitions of each table are shown in the next four screen shots; they all have an ID field of the AutoNumber type. If you need a quick refresher on building tables in Design view, look back at Chapter 8.

First, here's the Book table.

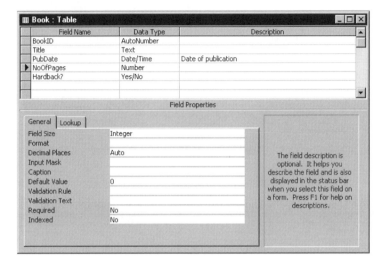

This is the Category table,

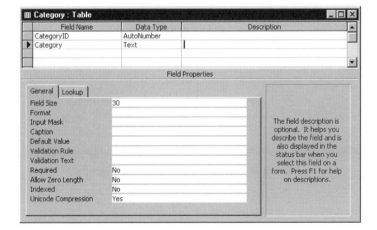

the Author table

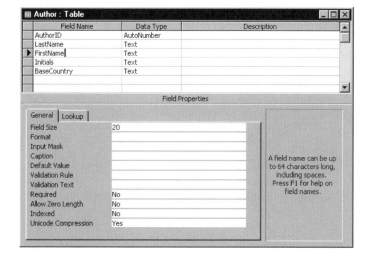

and the Publisher table.

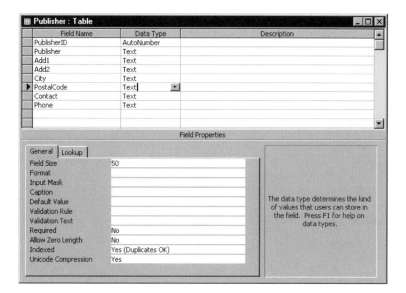

Adding primary keys

You'll probably be able to see where we're going with primary keys. In each table, the AutoNumber ID field is to be designated the primary key field. These are:

BookID in the Book table
CategoryID in the Category table
AuthorID in the Author table
PublisherID in the Publisher table

❦ *In reality you might choose to use a book's ISBN (International Standard Book Number) as its primary key, these being unique identifiers for almost all published material. They aren't quite universal but for a mainstream book catalog they'd do the job.* ❦

In Design view, highlight the field and click the Primary Key button.

Identifying foreign keys

In order to collate the record for a single book from the entries in all four tables, the Book table needs fields to act as foreign keys to the ID fields in the Author, Publisher and Category tables.

To the Book table definition in the Design view, add three fields of the Number: Long Integer type. It is common practice for these fields to bear the same name as their AutoNumber counterparts. This is not obligatory but using the same name does give a good indication of what the join is doing (for instance, matching AuthorID records in one table with AuthorID records in another).

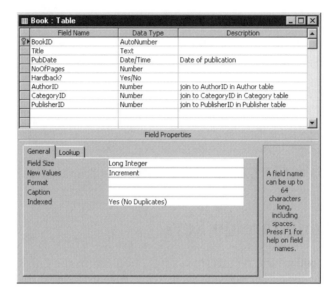

Joining the tables

Open the relationships window by clicking the Relationships button and then put the four tables in place.

Click on the AuthorID field in the Author table and drag it across to the AuthorID field in the Book table and drop it. Ensure that the correct fields and tables are identified in the Edit Relationship dialog, check the referential integrity box and click Create.

Repeat these steps to make the joins between the CategoryID fields in Book and Category and between the PublisherID fields in Book and Publisher.

The relationship window should look like this.

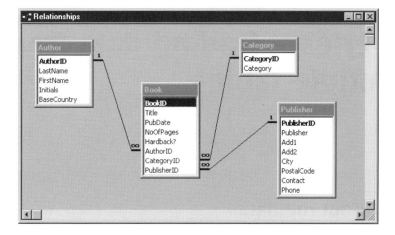

Objects

You may be wondering (worrying) about why we chose category as an 'object' worthy of a separate table. It is true that, in this simple example, we could have replaced the Category table with a lookup field in the Books table. In a real database there might be other properties associated with the different categories – color, size, packaging etc. We have included it here as a separate table simply to illustrate that objects, in terms of tables at least, aren't always physical objects.

Summary

The basic structure of the database is now complete; the tables have been built and the joins are in place between them. All it lacks is some data. Being the amiable types we are, you'll find a file called chap16end.mdb containing a database of an identical structure to the one described in this chapter and, what's more, it contains data. When you look at the table view of this data, you'll see that expand buttons appear alongside records in the Category, Publisher and Author tables, placed there automatically by Access.

Chapter 17

Queries – finding data from multiple tables

Check out the data

Take a few moments to look over the four tables in the Book database with
data (chap17start.mdb). Check out the Datasheet view of the Author
table: everything looks as you'd expect, including those useful expand
buttons in the first column. Click on one and, again as you'd expect, a
subtable pops out showing the related record or records from the Book
table (to which the Author table is joined). This is the first proof that the
joins in the new database are working: Access is using them to show you
related records.

❛ *This trick, new to Access 2000, is very neat and very useful for quick checks on
what's in a related table.* ❜

Having built a complete set of tables and allocated the data between them,
you now have a range of tables each of which holds only one aspect of the
whole catalog. For a human being interacting with the database, this could
perhaps be seen as less than ideal so a method is required to collate the data
into a complete record. This, as the chapter title implies, is done with
queries.

Bringing it all back together

A query can be based on one table or on many and building multi-table
queries differs not very much from building single table queries. We'll
build one now for showing complete records from the book catalog.

Multiple table queries

From the Queries tab in the database window, double click to build a new query in Design view. From the Show Table dialog, select all four tables (select the first in the list and Shift-Click on the last to select them all, then click Add). In the Table/Query pane you'll see the tables are displayed with their joins represented as lines, just as they are in the Relationship window.

Turning to the Query Design pane, the quickest way to see all the fields is to double click on the asterisk line in each table, a short cut to adding all the fields in the table to the query. The result, however, isn't ideal.

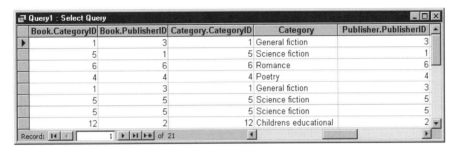

This shows part of the very wide answer table which contains several columns of extraneous information such as the ones shown above labeled `Book.CategoryID` and `Category.CategoryID`. These are displaying the ID fields from the `Book` and `Category` tables which isn't particularly helpful, especially as further along the answer table is a column labeled `Category` containing the type of book in plain English. The same happens with publisher and author ID data.

❝ *When Access needs to differentiate between fields of the same name from different tables, it displays the field name preceded by the table name, the two names being separated with a dot. The answer table above has fields labeled* `Book.CategoryID`, `Book.AuthorID` *and* `Category.CategoryID`, *amongst others.* ❞

To build a more concise and user friendly answer table takes a little longer but is well worth the effort. Close this query without saving it and start again in Design mode, adding all four tables as before. This time select fields from each table, leaving out every field that ends with 'ID'.

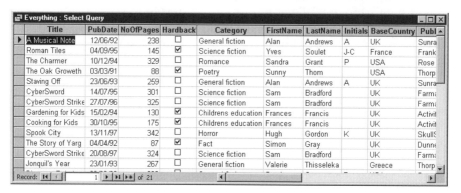

Title	PubDate	NoOfPages	Hardback	Category	FirstName	LastName	Initials	BaseCountry	Publ
A Musical Note	12/06/92	238	☐	General fiction	Alan	Andrews	A	UK	Sunra
Roman Tiles	04/09/95	145	☑	Science fiction	Yves	Soulet	J-C	France	Frank
The Charmer	10/12/94	329	☐	Romance	Sandra	Grant	P	USA	Rose
The Oak Groweth	03/03/91	88	☑	Poetry	Sunny	Thom		USA	Thorp
Staving Off	23/06/93	259	☐	General fiction	Alan	Andrews	A	UK	Sunra
CyberSword	14/07/95	301	☐	Science fiction	Sam	Bradford		UK	Farma
CyberSword Strike	27/07/96	325	☐	Science fiction	Sam	Bradford		UK	Farma
Gardening for Kids	15/02/94	130	☑	Childrens education	Frances	Francis		UK	Activit
Cooking for Kids	30/10/95	175	☑	Childrens education	Frances	Francis		UK	Activit
Spook City	13/11/97	342	☐	Horror	Hugh	Gordon	K	UK	Skulls
The Story of Yarg	04/04/92	87	☑	Fact	Simon	Gray		UK	Dunne
CyberSword Strike	20/08/97	324	☐	Science fiction	Sam	Bradford		UK	Farma
Jonquil's Year	23/01/93	267	☐	General fiction	Valerie	Thisseleka		Greece	Thorp

Record: |◄ ◄| 1 |► ►| |►*| of 21

The resulting answer table is still rather wide but its contents are a lot easier to understand. You can see complete records without any of the ID numbers that are primarily for use by Access rather than by users.

This query can also be created using the wizard: the choice of tools is up to you. I've saved this query, calling it `Everything`.

The rest of this chapter goes into more detail about querying multiple tables, different types of join, basing queries on other queries and so on. However, we have already covered the most important lesson that you can learn about querying multiple tables – which is that it is amazingly easy to do. And not only that, the result is also amazing. In earlier chapters we have shown you how to split the data up so that it is placed neatly in the separate tables. This query pulls it together again with Access doing most of the work for you. It is automatically matching all of the data in the primary and foreign keys; you don't need to tell it to do so explicitly. With a trivial amount of work you can pull the data that you need from the tables and see it in a way that is intuitively easy to understand.

As long as that message is clear, you have already understood most of what this chapter has to offer. Clearly we think the rest of the chapter is worth reading (it wouldn't be here if we didn't) but it is icing on the cake. However, icing is well worth having so let's look at that now.

The effect of joins on queries

The data that the query places in the answer table is selected on the basis of the joins present between the base tables (`Book`, `Author` etc.). When you create a join between two tables in the Relationship window, unless you specify otherwise, that join is what is called an Inner join. When we showed you the Relationship window (Chapter 15) we didn't show you how to create any other type of join apart from Inner because, as a good general rule, you don't often use any other type. Why? Because if you use an Inner join in the relationship window, you can always modify that at query time if need be. Of course, now that we've said that, you want to know what the possible variants are. Fine, no problem.

Inner join

The queries we've demonstrated in the book thus far look for matching data in the fields at either end of the join and, when a match is found, the record is popped into the answer table. So, if the value in the primary key matches the one on the foreign key, the data from the two records appears in the answer table. Conversely, if there's no matching data, there will be no record in the answer table.

This 'normal' type of join is properly called an inner join and is the default join type, always combining two or more tables on the basis of identical values within joined fields. It works well and is extremely useful but there may be occasions when you want something different.

Into the `Category` table you have entered all the likely classifications of book in the catalog. Suppose that, having also entered some book records, you want to see if there are any categories that are not represented by the current collection of books. If we use an inner join in the query, unallocated categories won't show up in the answer table from a query because, despite having a `CategoryID` number in the `Category` table, they have no matching records in the `CategoryID` field in the `Book` table. To produce the answer table you want, you need an outer join.

Outer join

If you use an outer join between the tables, the answer table generated by a query will let you see **all** the records in the table on one side of the join, even if there is no match in the other table.

In fact, to be pedantic, there are two types of outer join, depending on which records you wish to see in their entirety. The proper names for these flavors of outer join are 'left outer join' and 'right outer join' (although people often leave out the 'outer' part of the description and talk about left and right joins). The terms 'left' and 'right' come from the syntax used in the SQL querying language. The good news is that these translate very well into the Access query builder which makes left and right joins delightfully simple to use. However, this is probably getting far too theoretical and a demonstration should make it all clearer.

Create a new query in design view and add the tables `Category` and `Book`. Select the fields `Category.Category` and `Book.Title`.

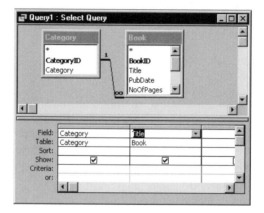

This is using the default join type, inner (which it is taking from the relationship window), so when we run it we see all of the books, each with its category.

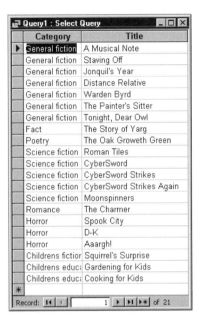

But we want to see which categories aren't used. So go back to the query and double click on the line that joins the two tables. This dialog should open up.

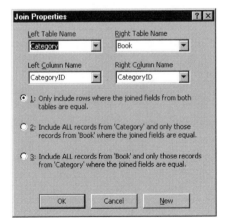

This shows the Join Properties of which there are three, all described in the dialog box in plain English.

1. The first is the default, the workhorse inner join. Hopefully, you will recognize it from the description given above.
2. The second type explains that it will give all the records from the `Category` table plus the matching ones from the `Book` table.
3. The third type is the reverse: all records from the `Book` table plus the matching ones from the `Category` table.

To get the result described above (all the categories regardless of whether or not the catalog contains books in each category) we want to use the type 2 join.

❢ *A type 3 join, in this instance, would give the same answer as a type 1 join because every record in the Book table has been allocated a category though, of course, this won't always be the case.* ❢

So, select the second option and click OK.

In the query window, the line depicting the join has changed subtly to include an arrowhead at the `Book` end of the join.

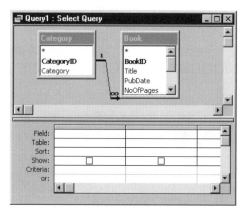

Run the query and...

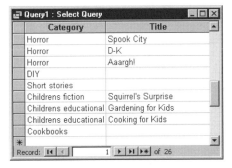

there are all the category records, most of them with associated book titles but some of them without. Just from this portion of the answer table we can see that there are no cookery books, short stories or books in the DIY category. This query is saved as `AllCats`.

Now we have demonstrated the left outer join and that is, theoretically, the end of the demo but we can't bear to leave it at that because you're probably wondering 'But how do I get a list which shows just the categories that aren't used?' This has nothing to do with left outer joins, but it's a good question and we can answer it using information you already have about queries. All we need to do is to add a condition to the query which says 'Show me this same list, but only include the records where the entry for the field `Book.Title` is null (that is, where there isn't a book title).' This is easily achieved by adding an 'is null' operator under `Book.Title`

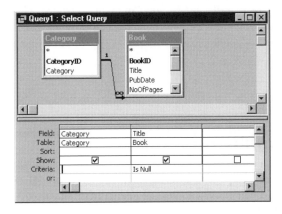

which produces:

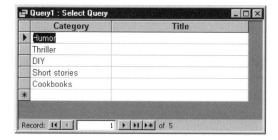

As we said above, the right outer join (showing all books) is, in this instance, the same as an inner join because all books have categories. However, as you start to build more complex databases the distinction between left and right outer joins can become useful. The important take-home message from this exercise is that Access normally returns all records where the values in the primary and foreign key match. On those occasions when you want to see values that don't have a match in the other key, you can use an outer join. This query is saved as UnusedCats (which sounds rather sad to an animal lover, but never mind).

❛ *There may come a time during your experimentation with joins and queries when you produce an answer table with many more records than you expect. The reason, almost certainly, is that the query has produced a Cartesian product. This grand name means that there were no joins between the tables in your query definition and when asked to perform a query based on unjoined tables, Access tries to help by working out all the possible permutations. Six records in one table and 16 in a second gives 96 records (6 × 16 = 96), most of them nonsense. This can become more serious with large tables. Given 10,000 records in each, the answer table will have 100,000,000 records.... The only thing to do is to go back to design, install some joins and rerun the query.* ❜

Basing a query on a query

As mentioned in Chapter 9, queries can be based on other queries. This is often an efficient approach, especially with multi-table queries which take a little longer to set up than those based on single tables.

I already have the Everything query to hand so when I want to find out in which countries authors are based and also in which country the publishers of their books are located, I can base a new query on `Everything`. Below is shown the new query, called `Geography`, which is based on that `Everything` query and with the records sorted by author last name:

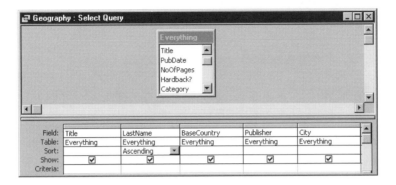

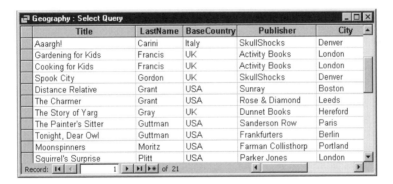

It's a quick and easy way to generate the answer, so when you need a new query, consider whether you have an existing one that can be pressed into service like this.

Summary

Queries in multi-table databases are even more flexible than they are in single table databases as you can 'mix and match' data from the various tables to reach precisely the information you want. All the different types of queries covered in Chapter 9 (range, update, crosstab and so on) are, of course, still available to you.

A query can either take all the records that have matching records in the tables to which they are joined or, using outer joins, you can insist that all records from a specific table are included in the answer table. Queries can be based on one table, all tables or a subset of tables and, by recycling an existing query as the basis for another, you can work even more efficiently.

The queries described above are to be found in the `chap17end.mdb` file.

Chapter 18

Forms – your interface to multiple tables

Forms and functions

So far you've only seen data from the `Book` multi-table database from the viewpoint of query-generated answer tables. This is fine for development work by people with an intimate understanding of the data but isn't half so fine for anyone expected to use the database simply as a tool. Users need to enter new records, browse and update existing records and be able to do this while looking at a pretty face.

Forms provide the pretty face and hide the excessively databaseish appearance of tables of raw data from the squeamish. Forms also have several neat ways of presenting data that can make life easy for users; chief among these is the subform.

Subforms

Consider the outer join query we built at the end of the last chapter. It shows each category of books together with the books in each category. A form with a subform is an ideal mechanism for displaying this information because it lets you see the category record as well as the related book records. Furthermore, the book records are presented in a way that makes it easy to browse through them. We could expend hundreds of words explaining what a subform is, but it's easier to show you.

Creating a form with a subform

Let's do this first with the Form wizard, working with the file `chap18start.mdb`. Launch the wizard and in the first step, select the

`Category` table and, from that, choose the `Category` field. Switch to the `Book` table and choose the `Title` field and then click the Next button. The second step looks like this:

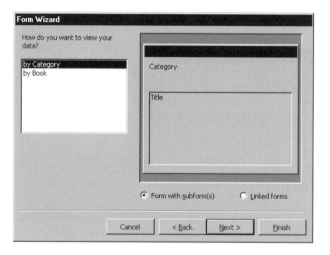

The wizard has determined that a subform is likely to offer the best view of the fields you've chosen and is asking whether you wish to view them by category or by book. The default has the 'by Category' option selected and in the preview panel to the right, you can see that the category will be shown at the top of the form with the book titles listed in a subform. If you move the highlight to 'by Book', you'll see that the wizard thinks a single form would display the records in their best light. However, we're here to inspect subforms, so return to the 'by Category' selection and click Next.

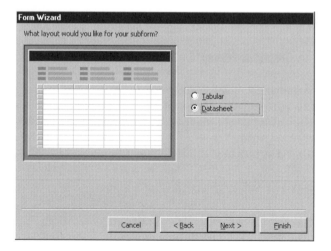

Pick a layout for the form: Tabular and Datasheet options are displayed. It's the layout for the book records on the subform that you're choosing here: as you can see from the preview, both options retain the records on the main form (the category records in this case) at the top of the form. I'll go with Datasheet and click Next.

Pick a style, in the final step give names to the form and subform (these are `AllCategories` and `BookSub`) and click Finish.

This is the resulting form.

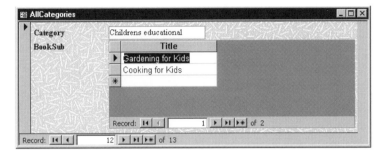

The category is shown at the top of the form and controls for moving through the category records are at the bottom of the form. In the subform, book records are shown, again with controls below.

You can base a form like this on more than two tables, for instance, a subform can display records from both the `Book` and the `Author` tables. The step defining the subform looks like this:

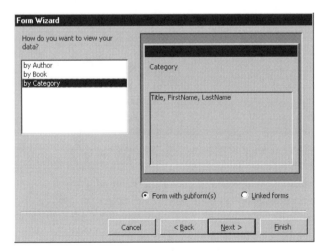

and the resulting form/subform like this:

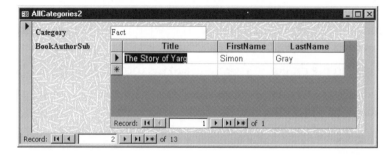

This form is called `AllCategories2` and the subform, `BookAuthorSub`.

❛ *Choosing memorable names for forms and subforms is quite important because after only a short period of experimentation, you can find the Forms tab bursting with forms. Remembering the relationships they have to each other can be tricky without hints from their names.* ❜

You can move the order of fields in the subform by clicking on the header when the cursor shows as a broad down arrow to select the whole column in the subform. Now you can click and drag the selected column to a new location. The layout will be saved whenever you close the `AllCategories2` form, an action which also closes the `BookAuthorSub` subform.

Note that when you use the form, you can edit all of the fields, including those in the subform. You can even add a `Category` but you can't add a book: a little thought tells you why.

❛ *I hate books that say that, it always implies to me that the authors don't understand it either. So, the reason is that the subform isn't showing all of the information necessary to ensure that all of the records are complete. If Access let you add a book you would end up with strange incomplete records. And, in practice, deciding which records can be updated/added is more taxing than it first appears for any RDBMS (Access included) so they tend to err on the side of caution.* ❜

That's really clever, but what happened?

This wizard is very powerful (clearly a member of some inner circle of magicians) by which we mean that it makes a complex process really easy. To use the wizard you don't have to know how it works. On the other hand, you may be curious to know how this form and its subform are working together. So that's what we are going to explain in this section but feel free to skip it for now (or for ever) if you aren't interested in the underlying mechanism.

If we take the first example, the wizard created two forms – AllCategories and BookSub. If you open the form BookSub on its own, you'll find that it's a fairly basic form that displays the Title field from Book as a datasheet. Note that it shows all of the books, not those associated with any particular category. So, when this form is used as a subform in the form called AllCategories, something in that form must be doing the clever work.

So, open up the form AllCategories in design mode and open up the properties window. Now click once (very carefully) on the subform so that it is highlighted with handles around the edge and so that the properties window reads Subform/Subreport: BookSub. (Double clicking on the subform won't give exactly this selection. If you get it wrong, click off the subform and try again.)

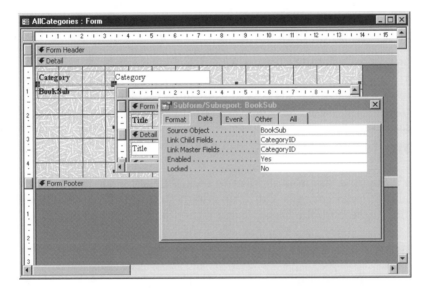

The Data tab of the properties window shows how the two forms are linked. The CategoryID field in the Book table (the Link Child Field) is being used to select the records in the book table that match the CategoryID field in the Category table (the Link Master Field).

❻ *Since the property window doesn't show the table names associated with the* CategoryID *fields, you might wonder how I know which is the master and which the child. The answer is that the link child field always comes from the subform.* ❾

OK, that's the end of the mechanics.

Another form based on multiple tables

Subforms aren't the only way of viewing data from multiple tables on one form. The other very commonly used method is to base a form on a query. The query pulls together records from multiple tables (from two or up to as many as there are in the database) and a form is then based upon that query.

If you base a form on the AllCats query, you can navigate through all the records and see the title of each book and its category.

When you're designing a form, the use to which it is to be put should be the deciding factor. The subform gives more of an overview while the simple form shown above lets the user concentrate on one record at a time.

More form controls

Now's the time, as promised at the end of Chapter 11, to introduce the remaining form controls. Returning with subform theme, we'll look at creating these from the Design view rather than from the Form wizard.

Subform/Subreport control

This example is to show the author on the main form and details of the books the author has written and their categories on the subform.

From the Form tab in the database window, click New, select Design View and the `Author` table.

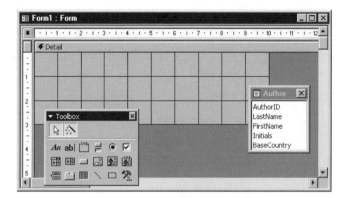

You should see a field list on the screen (as above) showing the fields in the `Author` table; if you don't, click the Field List button on the main button bar. Click on the `LastName` field and drag it onto the Detail section.

After checking that the Control Wizards button at the top of the Toolbox is selected, click on the Subform/Subreport button

in the Toolbox and drag to outline a rectangle on the Detail section. When you release the mouse button, the SubForm wizard starts up and asks whether the data for the subform is to come from existing tables and queries, or from an existing form. The records I want to see are in the `Book` and `Category` tables, so click the top option button and click Next. Select the `Book` table and move the `Title` field into the Selected Fields list. Now select the `Category` table and move the `Category` field across.

Click the Next button. Here you determine how the records in the main form are linked to those in the subform; the default is to display a list of options, as shown here.

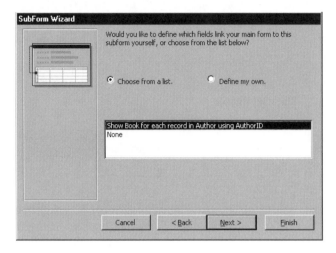

For this example, the first entry in the list sounds fine, selecting the records from the Book table on the basis of the AuthorID field.

❧ *If the wizard's suggestions don't suit, click the 'Define my own' option and set the fields for the form and subform as appropriate. You may have to go back a step to add the fields you need for linking purposes if these don't already figure as fields to be displayed in the subform.* ❧

Click Next and name the subform in the final step, clicking Finish thereafter. This is the Form view of the new form with its subform.

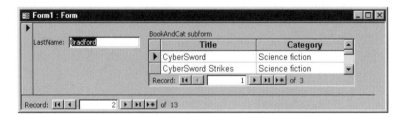

❧ *To see the subform clearly, you may need to flip into Design view and stretch the Subform control to a different shape.* ❧

With the browsing controls at the bottom of the form you can move between author records and as you do so, the relevant book and category records are shown in the subform. Further browse controls let you move through these records too.

List Box control

List boxes are especially useful on forms used for entering new data where they can eliminate misspelled words and inappropriate entries. The list box shows the user a list of all the possible entries for a field; picking one will fill in the field accurately. This is an example of how a list box on a form can look:

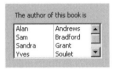

In many cases, the list that appears in the list box will be taken from an existing table though it is possible to type in a list of entries when you create the list box using the wizard.

The example below builds a form called `AddNewBook` for entering new book records. It will use three list boxes for entering the category, author and publisher for each new book. In each case, we want to ensure that details of the author and publisher are already stored in the database and that the book falls into an existing category.

From the Form tab in the database window, click New, select Design View and the `Book` table. From the Field List add the `BookID`, `Title`, `PubDate`, `NoOfPages` and `Hardback?` fields to the Detail section of the new form.

Now click on the List Box control in the Toolbox

and drag an outline for it on the form. The first step of the List Box wizard offers three options for the location of the values to appear in the list. The top option finds them in an existing table or query and is the default; it's also the one we want.

Click Next to choose the table or query containing values for the list; this list box will let users select a book's category so here it's the `Category` table.

Click Next and add the `Category` field to the Selected Fields list and click Next.

In fact, the `CategoryID` field has been added too by the wizard as you can see by going Back a step or by clicking to deselect the 'Hide key column (recommended)' check box.

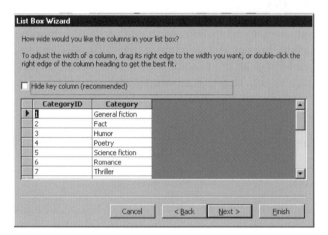

This is a sensible action by the wizard because it is the `CategoryID` field that is the basis for the link between the `Book` and `Category` tables. Click to reselect the option to hide the key column because, in the finished list box, you'll want users to see the categories in plain English, unencumbered by the ID number that exists primarily so that Access can ensure data integrity.

Click Next. When a user chooses a category when entering a new record, this information needs to be transferred into the right field in the `Book` table for storage. Of the two options offered, the second one fits the bill. Select the `CategoryID` field from the pop down list of fields (list boxes get everywhere!) in the `Book` table

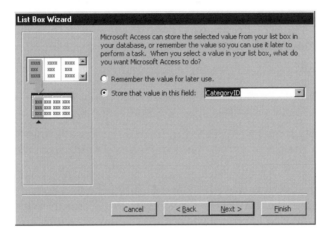

and click Next. Lastly, type in a label for the list box (something like 'Select a category' would be helpful to users) and click Finish.

This is the Form view of the new list box. If there are more values than will fit in the space allocated to the list box in the Design view, slider bars are provided automatically so you can scroll through the values.

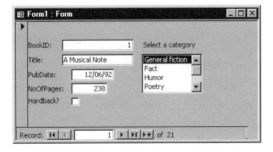

Flip to Design view to resize the rectangle that the list box inhabits and to move and resize the label if necessary.

That's really clever, but what happened?

Once again, you don't have to read this section, but do if you want to know how it works.

In Design view, let's look at some of the properties the wizard has set during the creation of this list box. I've set the Name property to `CategoryList`. The Row Source Type indicates that the values for the list are taken from a Table or Query and the Row Source identifies these.

What it shows you is, in fact, an SQL statement:

```
SELECT [Category].[CategoryID],
   [Category].[Category] FROM Category;
```

This is simply a query expressed in formal database terminology and the query finds the `CategoryID` and `Category` fields from the `Category` table.

The Column Count is two (the wizard added the `CategoryID` field after you'd selected the `Category` field) but the Column Widths property shows that the first column (`CategoryID`) has no width and is therefore hidden.

The Bound Column is shown to be column 1 (the first column), meaning that the `CategoryID` column in the list box definition is bound to the field specified in the Control Source property, in this case the `CategoryID` field in the `Book` table (you can tell it's from the Book table by popping down the list of fields). When a category is selected from the list box, its category ID number is stored in the `CategoryID` field in the `Book` table (i.e. in the Control Source).

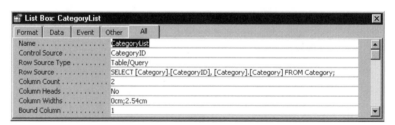

More list boxes

Now build another two list boxes to list the authors and the publishers. For the author list, choose the first and last name fields and, in the fourth wizard step, make the column widths 'best fit' by double clicking on the right edge of the columns. Store the value in the `AuthorID` field in the `Book` table. For the publisher list, the value should be stored in the `PublisherID` field in the `Book` table. Click the Save button and give the new form a name like `AddNewBook`.

Your form should now look like this:

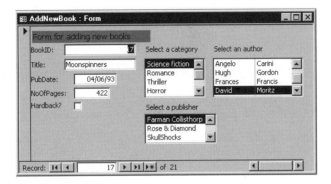

I've added a label to tell users what they can do from the form and now it's ready for testing.

❛ *It's not possible to test the form by adding a new record with just the category list box in place because of the joins that exist between the tables. Access would quite rightly object that there was no author and no publisher specified for the new book record and would not allow you to store an incomplete record.* ❜

Click the new record button and start by typing in a title for the new book (it gets an ID number automatically), a publication date, a number of pages and check the box if it's a hardback. Select a category by highlighting the one you want from the category list,

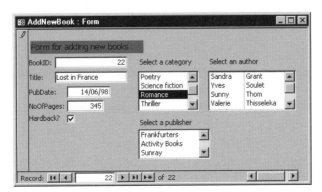

and an author and publisher from the remaining lists. Click in the narrow vertical pane to the left of the form and the tiny pencil graphic changes to an arrowhead to indicate that the new record has been successfully saved. Close the form and open the `Everything` query.

As you can see, the new book is in place with the category, author and publisher details in full, put in place by simple selections from list boxes.

Here's one final tip for using list boxes: to reach an entry quickly, type its first letter. Click anywhere in the list, type in 's' and the highlight zaps to 'Science fiction'; press 's' again to work through multiple entries beginning with that letter.

Combo Box control

A combo box is very like a list box but it has different strengths. It too presents a list from which values can be chosen but the list is not shown on the form until you ask to see it. A combo box looks like this

and when you click the button, the list appears.

One advantage of combo boxes is that they take up less room on a form, so if a form already has many controls on it, consider a combo box instead of a list box. Combo and list boxes behave in the same way, letting users select a value from a predefined list usually taken from a table or query, and storing it in the appropriate field. Combo boxes, however, will also allow values that do not appear in the list to be typed in.

❝ *The 'combo' in this control's name comes from its behavior which combines that of a list box (from which you can only select predefined values) and a text box (into which you can type new values).* ❞

We'll build a combo box on a form called AddNewPub that lets users add new publisher details to the Publisher table and with it users can either pick a city from the list or type in a new location.

The combo box will be based on a query rather than on a table so the first step is to build a query that simply pulls out all the records from the City field in the Publisher table. We can, at the same time, get the query to sort them in alphabetical order. This isn't essential, but people generally like sorted lists of information, so we might as well make life easy for them. The answer table looks like this:

which isn't ideal because London figures twice and the list we want for the combo box shouldn't contain duplicates. (Such a list *can* contain duplicates but for efficient use values should appear once only).

In Design view of the query, click anywhere on the Table/Query pane background and click the Properties button from the main button bar. In the list of Query Properties is a property called Unique Values, presently set to No. Set this to Yes

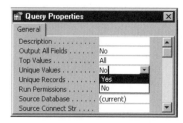

and take another look at the Datasheet view. London no longer appears twice in the list. Close this query, saving it as `Cities`.

In the Form tab of the database window, click the New button, select Design View and the `Publisher` table. Add all the fields from the property list except the `City` field. Click the Combo Box button in the Toolbox

and drag an outline onto the form. In the first step of the Combo Box wizard, choose the first option, that of looking up values for the list in a query or table. Click Next and click the Queries option in the View panel to see your saved queries.

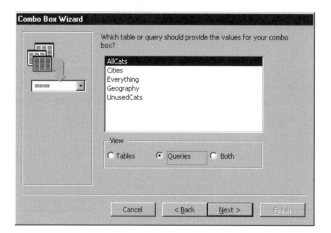

Double click the `Cities` query (or highlight it and click Next). In the next two steps, select the one and only field and alter the column width to suit. Then specify the `City` field as the field in which to store the chosen value and lastly choose a label for the combo box.

This is the Form view of the new control when entering a new publisher. A click pops down the list or you can start typing a new entry in the text box. If you start typing a value that already appears in the list, that value is popped automatically into the text box. Typing a 'D' pops Denver in;

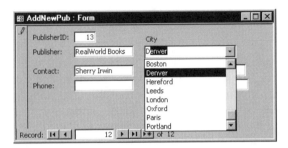

if you then type an 'e' and a 't', the text box clears, leaving you to type 'roit' to add the city of Detroit. The next time you open the `AddPub` form to add a new publisher, the query runs and generates a list that includes the new value for Detroit.

❦ *Note how carefully we phrased that. If, after adding Detroit and without closing the form, you enter another new publisher and pop down the list, Detroit won't appear. This is because the query to find all of the cities runs when the form is opened, not every time you use the combo box. This is not a bug, it's a feature. No, really, it is a feature! Most of the time people don't add new items when using a combo box and if the query ran every time the combo box was used, it would be slower. In fact, using the advanced features of Access (the programming bit) it is possible to re-run the query when an item is added but that falls outside the remit of this book. However, this is a good illustration of why Access has a programming language.* ❧

Tab control

Tab controls are useful for organizing forms by grouping related controls. A tab control looks like this:

To move between tabs you just click on the one you want, just as you do when inspecting the various types of property in the Property window. Tab controls are invaluable on forms that need to hold large amounts of data. Indeed, it is quite common to make the entire form a huge tab control so that all of the data that the user sees is inside one tab or another. On the sort of form we are using here, a tab control is probably over-kill but it demonstrates the principle.

We'll build a tab control into a variation of the `AddNewBook` form: start by making a copy of this form and calling it `AddNewBookTab` by highlighting the form in the database window, clicking the Copy and Paste buttons and typing in the new name. Now open the new form in Design mode.

Click on the Tab Control button in the Toolbox

and drag an outline onto the form. A tab control with two pages is now in place. First we'll change the page labels. At present each shows an arbitrary page number, the value of which will depend on how much experimentation you've done in your database.

Inspect the properties (click on the tab itself rather than on the body of the tabbed page) and you'll see that the page number appears as the Name property by which Access identifies the page object internally: it's advisable to change this to something by which you can identify it yourself. Now add a Caption property to appear on the tab; type what you want and the width of the tab is altered automatically to fit. My first tab is for BookDetails and this will work as a Name and, with a space, as a Caption.

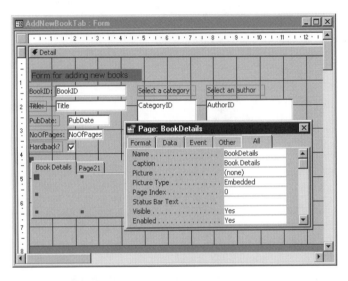

Controls can be placed directly on each page of a tab control in the same way as they can onto a form and existing controls can also be cut and pasted from the form onto a tabbed page.

❢ *Don't try to drag and drop existing controls from the form onto a tab control page. If you try it you'll find that when you let go of them, they apparently disappear because they have dropped, not onto the tabbed control page, but onto the form underneath. It is easier to use cut and paste as described here.* ❡

Select the NoOfPages and Hardback? fields by rubber banding, cut the selection, click the tab itself rather than the body of the page (the Property window should be headed Page: BookDetails) and paste. Shuffle the fields around into the required positions. Rename the second tab as Publisher Details and move the PubDate and the Publisher list box controls onto it.

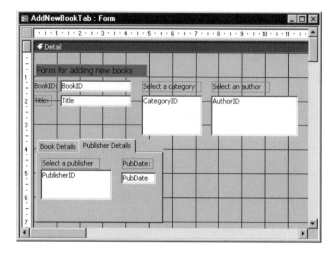

Flip into Form view and inspect the new control.

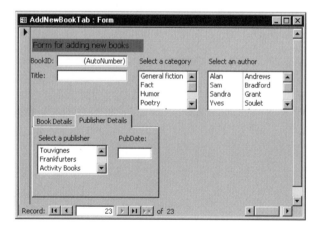

Back in Design view, you can add further pages by clicking with the right mouse button on the tab control. From the list that pops out, select Insert Page and that's what happens.

❛ *If the tab control isn't wide enough to display all its pages, a navigation control is added automatically.* ❜

From this menu you can also delete a page (make sure the focus is on the correct page before you do this as there's no dialog to confirm the deletion) and change the order of the pages across the tab control. Select the Page Order option,

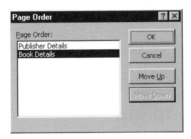

highlight the page to be moved and click the Move Up or Move Down buttons accordingly.

With the Tab Order option on this menu you can change the tab order within the current page of a tab control. To change the tab order of the tab control itself, right click anywhere on the form and select Tab Order.

Giving the tab control and its pages meaningful entries for the Name property pays dividends here: identifying Page18, Page19 and TabCtl4 can take some brain-racking.

Summary

With a grasp of the extensive armory of controls for Access forms, you can design and build forms for any purpose. Forms give users a helpful interface for entering data and for displaying it, either all records or a subset determined by an underlying query.

Try to think about a form from the users' point of view; keep things simple but don't hesitate to add helpful labels and captions. Use lines and rectangles to draw the eye towards groups of controls. Use the most appropriate control: a check box for a filling in a Yes/No field is quicker than selecting from a list. Use tab controls to give a logical flow to progress through the data entry process. Use list and combo boxes to control data entry and improve the integrity of your data.

The examples covered in this chapter all appear in `chap18end.mdb`.

Chapter 19

Reports – printing data from multiple tables

Basing reports on queries

Queries and reports are very much joint partners in the production of summarized information from your database. Each has an area of data handling where it performs best and together they give a high degree of control over report production. Queries are good at locating data that meets certain criteria. Reports are good at sorting and summarizing data, and at adding totals, subtotals, percentages, averages and so on.

For instance, a query can easily show authors based in the US, the books they've written and for which publishing houses, and while these can be sorted on the author's last name and then on the publisher, it takes more than a glance to see which authors have had books published by more than one publisher.

FirstName	LastName	BaseCountry	Title	Publisher
Sandra	Grant	USA	Distance Relative	Activity Books
Sandra	Grant	USA	The Charmer	Farman Collisthorp
Wayne	Guttman	USA	The Painter's Sitter	Parker Jones
Wayne	Guttman	USA	Tonight, Dear Owl	Touvignes
David	Moritz	USA	Moonspinners	Thorpes
Solomon	Plitt	USA	Squirrel's Surprise	Dunnet Books
Sunny	Thom	USA	The Oak Groweth Green	Sunray

AuthorPublisher : Select Query

Record: 1 of 7

A report based on this query (both query and report are called `AuthorPublisher` and are in the `chap19start.mdb` file) could display the data looking like this:

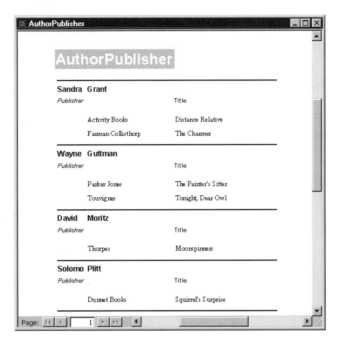

The records are still sorted by the authors' last name and by the publisher, but each author appears only once and the publishers are listed thereafter. Now it's much easier to see that Grant and Guttman have both published books with different publishers.

True, we've covered most of this information in Chapter 12 and there isn't much more to say here, so why this separate chapter? Well, one reason is symmetry – all of the other main components get their own chapter in the multi-table section. There is a danger that the reports will sulk if they don't get their own chapter. But fractionally more seriously we wanted to make the point that, once you start working with multi-table databases, queries become even more important when you create a report. Almost all reports in multi-tables databases are based on queries which gather the relevant data together from the separate tables.

That's the main take-home message. However, just to stop this chapter looking ridiculously short, we'll show you one more feature of reports that we like.

Adding a watermark

To add a bit of a dash, you can simulate a watermark on your reports very easily. Click the report selector and set the Picture property to the graphics file of your choice. The Build button lets you browse the various folders where clip art or your personal artwork is stored.

Set the Picture Type property to either linked or embedded. An embedded picture is stored in the database file; this is a good choice if the graphics file is on your personal hard disk and may not be accessible to anyone else using your database. So long as the graphics file is on your hard disk, you can use the linked setting.

You can experiment with the Picture Size Mode, Picture Alignment and Picture Tiling properties to get the effect you want. (Tiling only works with Clip and Zoom Picture Size Mode settings).

The watermark looks best if a pale colored design is used: it interferes less with the information displayed in the report.

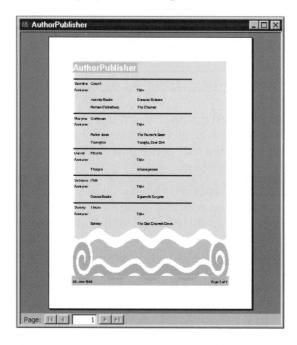

This jazzy report is called AuthorPublisherWatermark – another snappy name from your intrepid writers – and is in the chap19end.mdb file.

Summary

Having now completed a third pass through the four main elements of a database, you should have a clear picture of how Access can help you control the data that's stored in the database and also help you extract it in ways you find helpful. In the next chapter, we'll look at the database as a complete application.

Chapter 20

Producing a user interface for your database

Not just a pretty face

Your database needs to present an attractive, unified user interface (UI) to the world. This interface can ensure that users are able to perform the actions they want with the minimum of effort. A good UI has an uncluttered layout with informative labels and instructions to keep users on the right track. The paths through the application should also be plainly sign-posted, with options for retracing steps if a wrong choice is made and for exiting the application tidily.

All the tools you need to build a user interface to your database application are to hand in Access. In the main, you'll use the form controls introduced in Chapters 11 and 18 to create a series of forms that guide users through the necessary processes.

Design considerations

An entire book could be written about database UI design. However, the following pointers may help.

The main message is to keep it simple, avoiding too much color, too many different fonts, too many graphics and generally just too much on a single form. All these elements can, of course, be used most successfully in moderation. If, for instance, tasks divide straightforwardly between adding records and searching existing records, then using a different colored background to the forms dealing with the two types of task gives users an instant visual clue to where they are in the application. This also tells us that consistency of design is important. If you have a button for performing a common task (closing the application and/or closing Access, for instance) that you use on more than one form, put the button in the same place on each form.

❦ *When you have several forms that are largely similar, build one and make copies, editing the copies as necessary for their different roles. This cuts down the workload and also ensures a degree of consistency.* ❧

Consider the wording on your forms carefully. Will your users understand the terse instruction 'add record' or would 'add a book entry' be clearer?

The most common approach to designing a UI is to adopt a branching structure, starting with a main form from which a choice is made depending on the task in hand. Such a form is known as a switchboard.

Switchboards

A switchboard for the book database might lead on to forms for adding new records or searching for particular information.

Clicking on the lower button could lead to an option group which lets the user choose what sort of information to inspect.

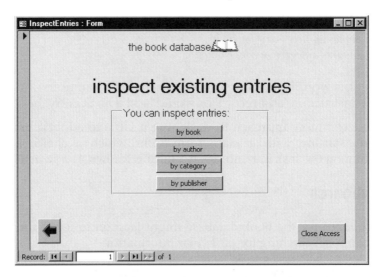

The switchboard form is often set to open automatically as soon as the database application is launched (which can be from a shortcut on the Windows desktop), leaving the user in no doubt about how to get started.

Form control without programming

Controlling the paths users can take through the forms that comprise a UI can, of course, be achieved by writing sections of Visual Basic code and attaching them to controls on the forms. With the more complex database applications this is usually how it is done. Happily you can get started without programming by using a combination of two simple ideas: one is that a command button can close the current form or open a new form and the second is that you have complete control over the size of each form.

On the switchboard the user has a choice of command buttons. If, for instance, the 'add new entries' button is clicked, a form opens from which new records can be added. Its size and position are carefully set so that it completely covers the switchboard form which remains open underneath (but cleverly concealed from sight). When the user clicks the command button to return to the switchboard, the current record-adding form closes and the switchboard form becomes visible again.

Thus, given buttons to open and close forms and with the judicious use of sizing, a seamless interface can be constructed. It does, of course, have its limitations. This method will work best with simple interfaces without branches at many different levels but it has the benefits of being quick and easy to build.

Designing a user interface

The first tools you'll need are good old fashioned pencil and paper. Think about what the users will want to do and how best to guide them. Circles, arrows and scribbled notes are a good way of organizing your thoughts and determining the likely paths through the application and thereby deciding upon how the interface will reflect this.

We've decided that our UI needs a switchboard and from the switchboard, users need access to two task areas – each of which has a form, one for adding new records and one for searching existing records. Below these two forms are further forms for performing specific operations. For ease of reference, we'll describe the switchboard form as being Level 1, the adding and inspecting forms Level 2 and the forms where entries are made or browsed Level 3.

			Switchboard				
	Add new records ↙				Inspect existing records ↘		
add new Book ↙	add new Author ↓	add new Category ↓	add new Publisher ↘	by Title ↙	by Author ↓	by Category ↓	by Publisher ↘

This diagrammatic representation shows the structure of the complete UI.

Once you start setting fingers to keyboard, it's best to work backwards, first building the Level 3 forms, then the Level 2 and finally the switchboard. Why this is so should become apparent as we work through the example.

Building an interface

We'll now take a gallop through the process of building this simple UI based on the Books database. Many of the steps you'll have seen before so we'll skim over much of the detail. In addition, we have part-built some of the forms for you so that you can concentrate on the parts that are novel: start from the `chap20start.mdb` file.

Level 3

Starting with Level 3 of the hierarchy in the UI diagram above, we've chosen two forms that we've already created in earlier chapters. One allows users to add a new book record to the database (`AddNewBook`) and the other allows them to look for books by specific category (`AllCategories2`). I've renamed the `AllCategories2` form as `InspectByCategory` so that its name reflects its role in the interface structure. The forms look like this:

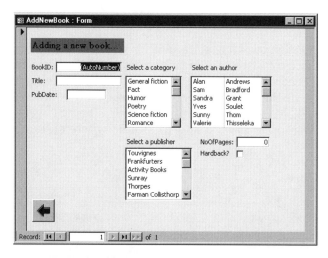

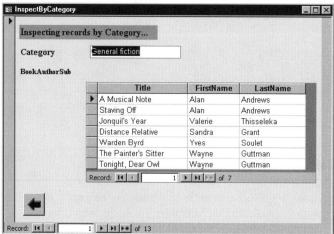

You could also either create new forms or identify other ones you may have already built during earlier sessions.

Both the forms shown above have a 'Back' button built with the Command Button wizard which, when clicked, closes the current form.

In the hierarchy described, there are six further forms at this level but these two should be enough to give you the idea.

Level 2

Below is the Design view of the part-built `AddEntries` form reached when the user chooses, at the switchboard, to add a new record.

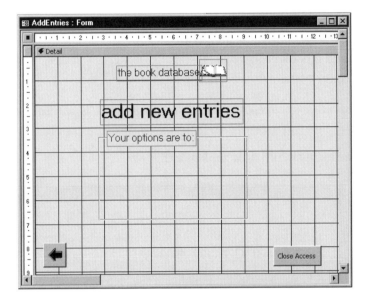

A small title banner with a graphic has been added and a larger label indicates the form's purpose. There are two command buttons, both built with the wizard. The Close Access button makes use of the Quit Application action from the Application category to do just what it says, and the Back button closes the current form. Lastly, there's an option group with a label.

❧ *Option groups, you'll recall, usually contain check boxes, option or toggle buttons, not command buttons. However, turning off the Control wizards in the Toolbox and putting an option group on the form is a very quick way of placing a box and label on your form which you're then free to fill with command buttons. You can, of course, build exactly the same look with the Rectangle tool and a Label, altering the format settings to get the same etched appearance etc.* ❧

What we need to add now are the buttons to open the Level 3 forms.

We have already covered the construction of command buttons, so add one, choosing the following options:

- Category – Form Operation
- Action – Open Form
- Form – AddNewBook
- Open the form and show all records
- Text – add a book entry
- Meaningful name – AddBook

❧ *The wizard only lets you choose from existing forms which is why working from the bottom up is such a good idea.* ❧

Great. The form should now look like this:

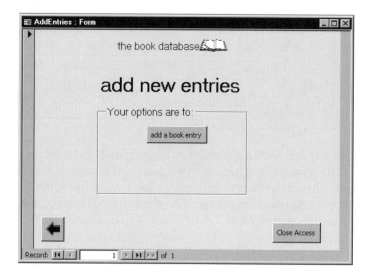

Save it and try it out. It works fine except when the AddNewBook form opens up it's showing all of the records, so the user will have to move to a new record before they can add one. Since this form now has one purpose in life (allowing users to add new books) we should be able to customize it for this purpose. Move to Design mode for this form, call up the properties for the entire form (click on the square at the top left of the form) and set the Data Entry property to Yes. This tells the form that it is to be used for data entry, so it won't bother showing any existing records.

Now the buttons and forms should work fine together. You can repeat the whole exercise for the `AddNewAuthor` form – that's in the file though we haven't included data entry forms for publishers or categories but you know everything you need to build these if you want to complete the application. The finished `AddEntries` form is shown below:

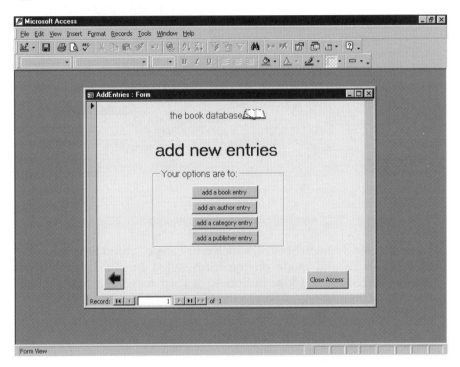

The `InspectEntries` form is largely similar with options for getting to the various browsing pages. Clearly you shouldn't set the Data Entry property of the `InspectByCategory` form to Yes. However, since this form is supposed to be used for viewing information only, you might want to set its Allow Edits, Allow Deletions and Allow Additions properties to No.

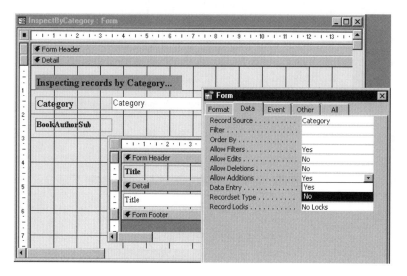

Level 1

Now let's tackle the switchboard, which is just a specialized type of form so start work in Design mode on the form called `Switchboard`. It has graphics, labels and a Close button so it's up to you to add the two command buttons to give access to the two Level 2 forms.

Click the Command Button tool and drag a rectangle out onto the form. In the wizard's steps, make the following selections:

- Category – Form Operation
- Action – Open Form
- Form – `AddEntries`
- Open the form and show all records
- Text – add new entries
- Meaningful name – AddNewEntries

Repeat these steps to create a second command button that opens the `InspectEntries` form.

I've also set the Format properties for Scroll Bars to Neither and for Navigation Buttons to No.

A seamless whole

Now you have to juggle with the form sizes so that the secondary forms, when open, completely cover the switchboard. The form property Auto Center is useful here as it ensures that a form always opens in the center of the screen. Set this property to Yes for all the forms in the UI. Then work your way through the various paths, dragging the forms to a size where they cover the underlying form: basically, the forms get larger as you work down the hierarchy.

❡ *You may find that you apparently resize a form and save it, but when you re-open it, lo and behold, it stubbornly returns to its original size. The trick is to open the form in design mode, and make sure that you resize the form itself (rather than alter the size of the window in which it appears).* ❡

If you want the switchboard to open automatically as soon as the book database is started, click Tools, Startup in the main menu bar. In the Startup window enter the name of the switchboard form (here it is Switchboard) under the Display Form/Page heading.

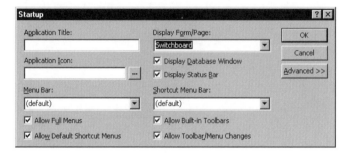

If you don't want to give users access to the database window, uncheck the Display Database Window option.

Further tweaks possible here are to type in the Application Title which will then appear on the top title bar that normally reads 'Microsoft Access'. You can also pick an icon for the application to appear instead of the Access key symbol in the title bar and so on.

A far from perfect UI

This user interface is a long way from perfect. All sorts of considerations haven't been explored:

- should you give users a button to click to save a record or can you rely on them being sufficiently Access aware to know that if they close a form the record will automatically be saved? Do they even need to worry about this?
- should you let users close Access or just close the database application?
- should users be forced to track back to the switchboard in order to exit?
- what about editing existing records?

The last point is an important one. At present there is no way for users to correct an entry that's incorrect. You may decide this doesn't matter, or maybe you don't want users editing records anyway. Or maybe you'll add a record editing option to the switchboard and another thread to the hierarchy.

Even when designing and building a simple UI there are many solutions, and it can be a time-consuming process. Guinea pigs are useful for testing the interface: what you think is obvious might be because of your high degree of familiarity with the system. Tactful, truthful and objective guinea pigs are ideal: failing those, grit your teeth and don't take criticism too personally!

Summary

Using these wizard-built buttons and the technique of opening and closing forms of carefully chosen dimensions, it's possible to put together an attractive and useable front-end to your database, tailored to the needs of your users. The user interface described above, so far as it goes, is in the `chap20end.mdb` file.

Chapter 21

You mean there's even more?

When Bill and I discussed this book, we were keen to try to actively pare down the information we included. So rather than tell you everything you could possibly need to know, we wanted to provide only the core information, enough to get you up and running as quickly as possible. This was because we felt that the very size and complexity of Access meant that there was a danger that new users of the product would get swamped by all of the detail. However, our approach makes it inevitable that we fail to go into detail about some of the more advanced facilities that Access offers.

This chapter, therefore, is designed to give you just a taste of Access' extras. We'll start with those three bottom tabs on the database window that we have stalwartly managed to avoid so far.

Pages – the webby bits of Access

As a very broad overview, a 'Page' is a web page that can be used to see (and manipulate) the data in an Access database.

Access, like the rest of the world, has become very web aware – if you aren't aware, you're square. There are, broadly, two places where people use web technology; on an intranet and on the Internet. In general terms, the web facilities that Access offers are aimed at intranet, rather than Internet use.

In Access 2000, the process of producing web pages is now an integrated part of the package rather than a feature with an add-on feel to it. In the database window you can choose to create a table, query, form or report – or a 'page'. The pages you can build are called, in Access terminology, data access pages, doubtless because this is their primary role in life. Data access pages are actually pages of extended HTML (HyperText Mark-up Language). In direct contrast to the other components of Access (tables, queries, forms and reports) these pages of HTML are not stored within the Access `.MDB` file. Instead each page is stored individually with an `.HTM` extension.

The accessing of data with a browser is nothing new but Access certainly makes it easy to implement browser access to a database. These new data access pages can maintain live links to data in the database and as such are ideal for letting intranet users see and, if you want them to, interact with up-to-date data.

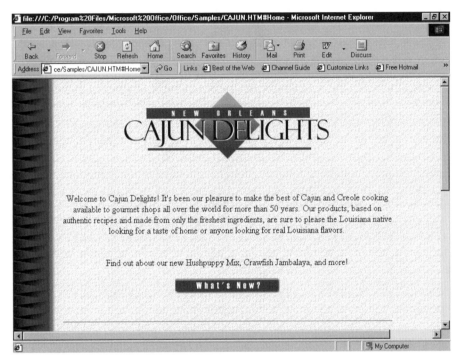

This is one of the sample data access pages supplied with Access. As you can see, very slick, professional-looking pages can be created.

Data access pages can either be designed from scratch with wizard help or not, or you can convert existing forms into HTML.

❡ *Internet Explorer 5 must be installed before you can work with data access pages.* ❡

Modules and macros

Access provides a host of ways to let you create databases without the need to become a programmer. However, if you really take to Access and start to develop more complex applications, there will doubtless come a point when you want the database to work in a particular way and there simply isn't a wizard available to help you to automate the process.

Microsoft provides a fully-blown programming language called Visual Basic (VB) inside Access which can be used to make the product do anything – dust the house, make tea, anything (OK, anything within reason). This is essentially the same language that's found in all of the Microsoft Office applications.

A module is simply a collection of pieces of code written in Visual Basic. These code snippets can either be associated with a certain Access report or form, or used throughout an Access application.

Access also allows you to create macros that can be used to automate processes within Access. Macros have a great deal of appeal because they give you some of the power of programming without actually having to program. A macro is built up from predefined actions, each of which performs a particular operation. Building a macro is, in fact, a very similar process to that of constructing a command button with the wizard, as covered in Chapter 11. The main difference is that you can choose from a larger number of actions to perform and that you are no longer limited to a single action per command button.

Macros are commonly used to automate actions that are repeated frequently, like running a report, printing it and closing it afterwards. A macro is often tied to a button which, when clicked, causes the macro to perform its actions.

So, if macros are so wonderful, why bother with VB? Well, macros are easier to learn than VB but not as versatile; some of the more complex operations that programmers perform with Access are impossible to perform from a macro. If you are really keen to take database development further, my advice is to take the plunge and learn Visual Basic.

Application development

Suppose that you build a database in Access for your department or company. It starts life as a simple application that you and perhaps one other person use. It sits on one machine so you take turns using the database. You both help to develop it, you both know it like the back of your hand, you can both use it effectively.

The database is so useful that it rapidly becomes important, not to say crucial, to the running of the organization. This is good, but you are likely to hit several distinct issues at about this time.

- What happens when untrained people start to use it?
- How do you let different people have different access to the database (perhaps some of them should only have the ability to read, but not alter, the data)?
- How do you allow between five and ten people to use the database at the same time from different machines?
- Does it matter if the number of people goes up to, say, 50?

What happens when untrained people start to use it?

They uncover all of the holes that you didn't know were there. **You** know how to use the database because you helped to design and build it. You instinctively know that you have to add an author to the author table before trying to add a book to the book table. It's obvious – but not to someone who has never used a database. So the users will need to be trained and the database may need some further development work.

How do you let different people have different access to the database (perhaps some of them should only have the ability to read, but not alter, the data)?

By making use of Access' security features which are designed for just this purpose.

Security is a broad subject with far-reaching consequences and in this book we only scratch at the surface. If your databases need sophisticated protection, however, it's likely that it can be set up just as you wish.

The simplest form of security is to assign a password to the database application: users must type in the password in order to access the database. This offers no protection to the database components: your table designs, queries and so on can still be altered by any user but only, of course, if that user has the password. For a home or small business database there are instances where this type of protection will be adequate.

An alternative is to opt for user-level security which can be used to limit the access users have to the components you have created. User-level security is extremely flexible, letting you determine exactly who can do what. You can set it up so that users cannot change the design of tables, that they have read-only access to queries (so they can see what they do but not alter them) and even so that they can't access certain tables of sensitive data (salaries information, for example) at all.

Anyone who uses the database is a user and has a name and a password. Each user is allocated to one or more groups and is said to be a member of a group or groups. Each group is given permissions that enable the users in the group to perform certain tasks. Access provides uses predefined groups include Read-Only Users, whose members can read all data but cannot alter it nor the design of any database object, and Full Data Users, who can edit the data but not alter the design of any database object.

In addition, there is a User-Level Security Wizard, accessed from the main menu under Tools, Security. This advanced wizard with many steps takes a lot of the sting out of a job that can be somewhat challenging.

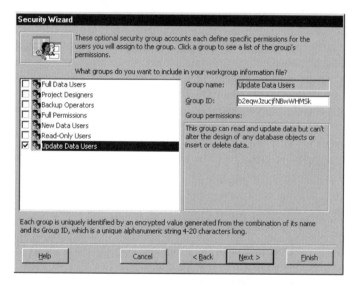

This is a typical page from the wizard. Here you determine which of the predefined groups you wish to use for the database. The groups have descriptive names indicating the sort of tasks users can perform and text to the right describes this in more detail.

When you set up a security system with this wizard, it produces a report outlining the security that has been put in place. Print this out and keep it safe as it contains information you'll need if you ever need to recreate this particular setup.

How do you allow between five and ten people to use the database at the same time from different machines?

Let's assume that all of the machines are networked and can all 'see' a common disk somewhere on the network. Let's further assume that all of the machines have a copy of Access 2000. If you put the Access .MDB file on the common shared disk then, if all is well, all of the users should be able to use the database at the same time. Note that tiny phrase slipped in there 'if all is well'. Sharing databases is much easier than it used to be but it still often requires a reasonable understanding of both networks and data-bases. However, the good news is that, possibly with a bit of initial tweaking, Access is capable of allowing multi-user access to data.

Does it matter if the number of people goes up to, say, 50?

Yes. The Access .MDB format allows multiple copies of Access to use the same database simultaneously. The mechanism that it uses to allow this is sub-optimal when the number of users increases above about ten (the actual number depends upon what those users are doing). 'Ah ha', you think, 'sub-optimal. That's code for badly designed.' Not really. Access was designed to be optimal when run as a stand-alone database engine and that was a sensible decision because that's the way it is normally used.

So, what do you do if you want lots of people to use the database? You upsize your Access application to some database engine that is designed for large numbers of simultaneous users. Such an engine might be Microsoft's SQL Server, or it could be Oracle's Oracle or IBM's DB2. These database engines sit, not on the PC, but on the server with the data. They can handle not just 50 simultaneous users, not just 500, not just 5,000... you get the picture. How you upsize the application is another book but all of these companies now offer wizards or the equivalent to help you upsize.

Which brings us neatly to project files.

Projects

Before describing an Access project, here's a little background to help give a context to the description.

At the core of Access lies what's known as a database engine. Called the Jet engine, it is software that keeps such things as referential integrity, valida-tion at the table level and joins between tables under control and it also performs whatever searches and queries are required by the users.

When you create an Access application within its .MDB file, your creation is optimized for use by the Jet engine. (Incidentally, isn't it a great name? It sounds like something from a Flash Gordon story, or at least from the archives of the Jet Propulsion Laboratory).

Microsoft's other RDBMS product, SQL Server, also has a database engine, but that is a very different beast, heavily optimized for multiple users.

Microsoft had the clever idea of coming up with a third engine called the MicroSoft Database Engine (MSDE, possibly to be renamed at the time of writing). This one is exactly the same as the SQL Server engine except that it will run on stand-alone PCs and is sub-optimal for more than about 10 users. 'Ah ha', you think again, 'sub-optimal. That's code for badly designed.' No, it was a decision taken by Microsoft in cold blood to actively and deliberately restricted this engine so that it doesn't work well with more than a few users. Why? Well, if you want to run with hundreds of users, Microsoft wants to sell you SQL Server. However, Microsoft also wants to give you a path to upsize easily from Access to SQL Server and therefore provides the MSDE.

When you elect to create an Access project, Access stops using the Jet engine and switches to the MSDE. You continue to use Access and it will apparently work in much the same way as before. You can use it to create tables, queries, forms and so on. In fact, the only major difference that you will notice at first is that when you create a new table, Access offers you a different set of data types. However, all of the work you do can later be updated to SQL Server really easily because the MSDE is really SQL Server by another name.

Project files have an .ADP extension instead of the usual .MDB extension. Unlike an .MDB file, a Project file contains no tables of data, just forms, reports, macros, modules and data access pages. The tables of data are looked after by the MSDE but, when viewed from Access running on a client machine, the tables are visible components just as they are in stand-alone Access applications.

Summary

There are other really interesting bits of Access but the areas in this chapter are those we would examine if we had read this book and wanted to know what to examine next. We hope you enjoy using Access as much as we have enjoyed our involvement with it.

Index

317